Genetics Experiments

FACTS ON FILE SCIENCE EXPERIMENTS

Genetics Experiments

Pamela Walker
Elaine Wood

Facts On File
An imprint of Infobase Publishing

Genetics Experiments

Facts On File, Inc.
An imprint of Infobase Publishing
132 West 31st Street
New York NY 10001

Library of Congress Cataloging-in-Publication Data
Walker, Pam, 1958-
Genetics experiments / Pamela Walker, Elaine Wood.
p. cm.— (Facts on File Science Experiments)
Includes bibliographical references and index.
ISBN 978-0-8160-8173-8
1. Genetics–Experiments. I. Wood, Elaine, 1950- II. Title.
QH440.4.W35 2011
576.5078–do22
2010019814

Facts On File books are available at special discounts when purchased in bulk quantities for businesses, associations, institutions, or sales promotions. Please call our Special Sales Department in New York at (212) 967-8800 or (800) 322-8755.

You can find Facts On File on the World Wide Web at http://www.factsonfile.com

All links and Web addresses were checked and verified to be correct at the time of publication. Because of the dynamic nature of the Web, some addresses and links may have changed since publication and may no longer be valid.

Editor: Frank K. Darmstadt
Copy Editor: Betsy Feist at A Good Thing, Inc.
Project Coordinator: Aaron Richman
Art Director: Howard Petlack
Production: Victoria Kessler
Illustrations: Hadel Studios
Cover printed by: Bang Printing, Brainerd, MN
Book printed and bound by Bang Printing, Brainerd, MN
Date printed: October 2010
Printed in the United States of America

10 9 8 7 6 5 4 3 2 1

This book is printed on acid-free paper.

Contents

Preface

For centuries, humans have studied and explored the natural world around them. The ever-growing body of knowledge resulting from these efforts is science. Information gained through science is passed from one generation to the next through an array of educational programs. One of the primary goals of every science education program is to help young people develop critical-thinking and problem-solving skills that they can use throughout their lives.

Science education is unique in academics in that it not only conveys facts and skills; it also cultivates curiosity and creativity. For this reason, science is an active process that cannot be fully conveyed by passive teaching techniques. The question for educators has always been, "What is the best way to teach science?" There is no simple answer to this question, but studies in education provide useful insights.

Research indicates that students need to be actively involved in science, learning it through experience. Science students are encouraged to go far beyond the textbook and to ask questions, consider novel ideas, form their own predictions, develop experiments or procedures, collect information, record results, analyze findings, and use a variety of resources to expand knowledge. In other words, students cannot just hear science; they must also do science.

"Doing" science means performing experiments. In the science curriculum, experiments play a number of educational roles. In some cases, hands-on activities serve as hooks to engage students and introduce new topics. For example, a discrepant event used as an introductory experiment encourages questions and inspires students to seek the answers behind their findings. Classroom investigations can also help expand information that was previously introduced or cement new knowledge. According to neuroscience, experiments and other types of hands-on learning help transfer new learning from short-term into long-term memory.

Facts On File Science Experiments is a multivolume set of experiments that helps engage students and enable them to "do" science. The high-interest experiments in these books put students' minds into gear and give them opportunities to become involved, to think independently, and to build on their own base of science knowledge.

As a resource, Facts On File Science Experiments provides teachers with new and innovative classroom investigations that are presented in a clear, easy-to-understand style. The areas of study in this multivolume set include forensic science, environmental science, computer research, physical science, weather and climate, space and astronomy and many others. Experiments are supported by colorful figures and line illustrations that help hold students' attention and explain information. All of the experiments in these books use multiple science process skills such as observing, measuring, classifying, analyzing, and predicting. In addition, some of the experiments require students to practice inquiry science by setting up and carrying out their own open-ended experiments.

Each volume of the set contains 20 new experiments as well as extensive safety guidelines, glossary, correlation to the National Science Education Standards, scope and sequence, and an annotated list of Internet resources. An introduction that presents background information begins each investigation to provide an overview of the topic. Every experiment also includes relevant specific safety tips along with materials list, procedure, analysis questions, explanation of the experiment, connections to real life, and an annotated further reading section for extended research.

Pam Walker and Elaine Wood, the authors of Facts On File Science Experiments, are sensitive to the needs of both science teachers and students. The writing team has more than 40 years of combined science teaching experience. Both are actively involved in planning and improving science curricula in their home state, Georgia, where Pam was the 2007 Teacher of the Year. Walker and Wood are master teachers who hold specialist degrees in science and science education. They are the authors of dozens of books for middle and high school science teachers and students.

Facts On File Science Experiments, by Walker and Wood, facilitates science instruction by making it easy for teachers to incorporate experimentation. During experiments, students reap benefits that are not available in other types of instruction. One of these benefits is the opportunity to take advantage of the learning provided by social interactions. Experiments are usually carried out in small groups, enabling students to brainstorm and learn from each other. The validity of group work as an effective learning tool is supported by research in neuroscience, which shows that the brain is a social organ and that communication and collaboration are activities that naturally enhance learning.

Experimentation addresses many different types of learning, including lateral thinking, multiple intelligences, and constructivism. In lateral thinking, students solve problems using nontraditional methods. Long-established, rigid procedures for problem-solving are replaced by original ideas from students.

When encouraged to think laterally, students are more likely to come up with unique ideas that are not usually found in the traditional classroom. This type of thinking requires students to construct meaning from an activity and to think like scientists.

Another benefit of experimentation is that it accommodates students' multiple intelligences. According to the theory of multiple intelligences, students possess many different aptitudes, but in varying degrees. Some of these forms of intelligence include linguistic, musical, logical-mathematical, spatial, kinesthetic, intrapersonal, and interpersonal. Learning is more likely to be acquired and retained when more than one sense is involved. During an experiment, students of all intellectual types find roles in which they can excel.

Students in the science classroom become involved in active learning, constructing new ideas based on their current knowledge and their experimental findings. The constructivist theory of learning encourages students to discover principles for and by themselves. Through problem solving and independent thinking, students build on what they know, moving forward in a manner that makes learning real and lasting.

Active, experimental learning makes connections between newly acquired information and the real world, a world that includes jobs. In the 21st century, employers expect their employees to identify and solve problems for themselves. Therefore, today's students, workers of the near future, will be required to use higher-level thinking skills. Experience with science experiments provides potential workers with the ability and confidence to be problem solvers.

The goal of Walker and Wood in this multivolume set is to provide experiments that hook and hold the interest of students, teach basic concepts of science, and help students develop their critical-thinking skills. When fully immersed in an experiment, students can experience those "Aha!" moments, the special times when new information merges with what is already known and understanding breaks through. On these occasions, real and lasting learning takes place. The authors hope that this set of books helps bring more "Aha" moments into every science class.

Acknowledgments

This book would not exist were it not for our editor, Frank K. Darmstadt, who conceived and directed the project. Frank supervised the material closely, editing and making invaluable comments along the way. Betsy Feist of A Good Thing, Inc., is responsible for transforming our raw material into a polished and grammatically correct manuscript that makes us proud.

Introduction

From a young age, students are conscious of their appearance. Parents and friends may point out eye-catching features or remark how that they resemble family members. These kinds of conversations lead to interest in the topics of genetics, the study of the inheritance of traits.

Genetics Experiments is one volume of Facts On File Science Experiments, a new multivolume set of books on various fields of science. The goal of this volume is to provide science teachers with 20 original experiments that convey basic principles of genetics and inheritance. The experiments are designed to help students understand the meaning of patterns of inheritance as well as the molecular basis of genetic traits. Each experiment in the book is a proven classroom activity that broadens understandings of both scientific facts and the nature of science. The investigations are appropriate for both middle and high school classes.

To accommodate the wide range of learning styles in students, experiments approach genetic topics from several directions. Some use modeling, manipulatives, and role-playing to help student understand the changes that occur in DNA and proteins. Others have students carry out "wet" experiments such as those in which they use actual DNA or mate fruit flies and observe their offspring.

To provide a basis for understanding genetics, the experiment "Cells in Mitosis" tutors students on the stages of mitosis, then has them observe cells in each stage. Students find out how minor changes in DNA can lead to big changes in a protein in "Amino Acids in Sickle Cell Anemia." In "Meiosis," students create clay models of oogenesis and spermatogenesis. "Inheritance of Traits" is an activity in which students play the roles of parents of fictitious offspring with traits determined by flipping "chromosomes." "Predicted and Actual Results of Genetic Crosses" is an experiment in which students predict the cross between two guinea pigs, then simulate the cross to find actual results.

In "Using Karyotypes to Diagnose Conditions," students cut out pictures of chromosomes, relying on chromosome size and banding patterns to find homologous pairs, then look for abnormalities in size and number. Students collect their own cells and use them as a source of DNA in "Extracting DNA From Cheek Cells." In "Chromosomal Mutations," students create models showing deletions, duplications, inversions, translocations, and reciprocal translocations.

The modes of inheritance are examined from several angles. In "Design an Organism's Traits," students learn about different modes of inheritance by examining the traits of fictitious organisms. "Genetics Learning Centers" gives students creative freedom to develop stations where other students can learn about different modes of inheritance.

Students design their own experiments to learn more about how dominant and recessive traits are passed from parents to offspring in "Inheritance of Taste." In "Pedigrees Show Traits Within Families," students trace the appearance of the trait in an extended family, then develop a pedigree of the trait.

Fruit flies are used to demonstrate genetic principles in "The Traits of Parents and Offspring Are Not Identical" and "Transmission of Sex-linked Mutations." The former demonstrates the law of segregation, while the latter focuses on the reasons sex-linked traits appear more often in males than females.

Students learn the details of DNA structure by creating a replica of the double helix in "Model of a DNA Molecule." "Introduction to Gel Electrophoresis" and "DNA Gel Electrophoresis" enables students to learn about the principles behind electrophoresis and use their knowledge to cut separate DNA fragments with restriction enzymes.

Students share their expertise on different uses of genetic engineering in "Genetic Engineering Presentation." "Genetic Engineering With Plasmids" demonstrates how restriction enzymes are used to remove a gene of interest from eukaryotic DNA so that it can be inserted into bacterial plasmid DNA. Students learn about the mechanisms that manage the activity of genes in "Control of Gene Expression."

Every student can benefit from an understanding of basic genetics. Some students may one day need to make life-altering decisions based on genetic counseling. Wood and Walker hope that this volume helps all students understand the role of DNA in their lives.

Safety Precautions

REVIEW BEFORE STARTING ANY EXPERIMENT

Each experiment includes special safety precautions that are relevant to that particular project. These do not include all the basic safety precautions that are necessary whenever you are working on a scientific experiment. For this reason, it is absolutely necessary that you read and remain mindful of the General Safety Precautions that follow. Experimental science can be dangerous and good laboratory procedure always includes following basic safety rules. Things can happen quickly while you are performing an experiment—for example, materials can spill, break, or even catch on fire. There will not be time after the fact to protect yourself. Always prepare for unexpected dangers by following the basic safety guidelines during the entire experiment, whether or not something seems dangerous to you at a given moment.

We have been quite sparing in prescribing safety precautions for the individual experiments. For one reason, we want you to take very seriously the safety precautions that are printed in this book. If you see it written here, you can be sure that it is here because it is absolutely critical.

Read the safety precautions here and at the beginning of each experiment before performing each lab activity. It is difficult to remember a long set of general rules. By rereading these general precautions every time you set up an experiment, you will be reminding yourself that lab safety is critically important. In addition, use your good judgment and pay close attention when performing potentially dangerous procedures. Just because the book does not say "Be careful with hot liquids" or "Don't cut yourself with a knife" does not mean that you can be careless when boiling water or using a knife to punch holes in plastic bottles. Notes in the text are special precautions to which you must pay special attention.

GENERAL SAFETY PRECAUTIONS

Accidents can be caused by carelessness, haste, or insufficient knowledge. By practicing safety procedures and being alert while conducting experiments, you can avoid taking an unnecessary risk. Be sure to check the individual experiments in this book for additional safety regulations and adult supervision requirements. If you will be working in a laboratory, do not work alone. When you are working off site, keep in groups with a minimum of three students per group, and follow school rules and state legal requirements for the number of supervisors required. Ask an adult supervisor with basic training in first aid to carry a small first-aid kit. Make sure everyone knows where this person will be during the experiment.

PREPARING

- Clear all surfaces before beginning experiments.
- Read the entire experiment before you start.
- Know the hazards of the experiments and anticipate dangers.

PROTECTING YOURSELF

- Follow the directions step by step.
- Perform only one experiment at a time.
- Locate exits, fire blanket and extinguisher, master gas and electricity shut-offs, eyewash, and first-aid kit.
- Make sure there is adequate ventilation.
- Do not participate in horseplay.
- Do not wear open-toed shoes.
- Keep floor and workspace neat, clean, and dry.
- Clean up spills immediately.
- If glassware breaks, do not clean it up by yourself; ask for teacher assistance.
- Tie back long hair.
- Never eat, drink, or smoke in the laboratory or workspace.
- Do not eat or drink any substances tested unless expressly permitted to do so by a knowledgeable adult.

USING EQUIPMENT WITH CARE

- Set up apparatus far from the edge of the desk.
- Use knives or other sharp, pointed instruments with care.

- Pull plugs, not cords, when removing electrical plugs.
- Clean glassware before and after use.
- Check glassware for scratches, cracks, and sharp edges.
- Let your teacher know about broken glassware immediately.
- Do not use reflected sunlight to illuminate your microscope.
- Do not touch metal conductors.
- Take care when working with any form of electricity.
- Use alcohol-filled thermometers, not mercury-filled thermometers.

USING CHEMICALS

- Never taste or inhale chemicals.
- Label all bottles and apparatus containing chemicals.
- Read labels carefully.
- Avoid chemical contact with skin and eyes (wear safety glasses or goggles, lab apron, and gloves).
- Do not touch chemical solutions.
- Wash hands before and after using solutions.
- Wipe up spills thoroughly.

HEATING SUBSTANCES

- Wear safety glasses or goggles, apron, and gloves when heating materials.
- Keep your face away from test tubes and beakers.
- When heating substances in a test tube, avoid pointing the top of the test tube toward other people.
- Use test tubes, beakers, and other glassware made of Pyrex™ glass.
- Never leave apparatus unattended.
- Use safety tongs and heat-resistant gloves.
- If your laboratory does not have heatproof workbenches, put your Bunsen burner on a heatproof mat before lighting it.
- Take care when lighting your Bunsen burner; light it with the airhole closed and use a Bunsen burner lighter rather than wooden matches.

- Turn off hot plates, Bunsen burners, and gas when you are done.
- Keep flammable substances away from flames and other sources of heat.
- Have a fire extinguisher on hand.

FINISHING UP

- Thoroughly clean your work area and any glassware used.
- Wash your hands.
- Be careful not to return chemicals or contaminated reagents to the wrong containers.
- Do not dispose of materials in the sink unless instructed to do so.
- Clean up all residues and put in proper containers for disposal.
- Dispose of all chemicals according to all local, state, and federal laws.

BE SAFETY CONSCIOUS AT ALL TIMES!

1. Cells in Mitosis

Topic

Cells show distinct changes as they go through the process of mitosis.

Introduction

When you look back at your baby pictures, it is clear that you are much larger than you used to be. In other words, you have grown. Growth is one of the characteristics of living things. In order to grow, you must make more cells by the process of *mitosis*.

Cells have life cycles that follow predictable patterns. Most of a cell's life is spent in a period of growth called *interphase*. Just before a cell undergoes mitosis, it makes a copy of its chromosomes. All of the cells in your body (except the reproductive cells) contain 46 chromosomes. Before a cell begins mitosis, it makes another set of these chromosomes. When the cell divides and forms two cells, each of the daughter cells receives a full complement of 46 chromosomes.

To facilitate the study of mitosis, scientists have divided the event into four phases: prophase, metaphase, anaphase, and telophase. During these stages, two small organelles called *centrioles* produce a *mitotic spindle* across the cell. The fibers in this spindle attach to the chromosomes and move them around. At the end of telophase, the cell undergoes *cytokinesis*, a process in which the cell pinches itself in half. In this experiment, you will examine the stages of mitosis.

Time Required

25 minutes for Part A
25 minutes for Part B

Materials

- textbook showing interphase and mitotic cells or access to the Internet

- ➼ scissors
- ➼ glue
- ➼ photocopy of Figure 1
- ➼ science notebook

Safety Note   Take care when working with scissors. Please review and follow the safety guidelines at the beginning of this volume.

Procedure, Part A

1. Use your textbook or the Internet to examine figures of cells in interphase and in the various stages of mitosis.

2. Answer Analysis questions 1 through 3.

3. Examine the cells in Figure 1, which show the stages of mitosis. These cells are not arranged in the order in which mitotic events occur. Using a photocopy of the figure, cut out and glue the cells to a sheet in your science notebook in the order given in the following descriptions:

   a. Interphase: The nuclear membrane surrounds the nuclear material. The nucleolus is present and looks like a dot in the nucleus. Centrioles, which look like small barrels, are present.

   b. Early prophase: The nuclear membrane is still in place. The nucleolus has disappeared, and the chromosomes have thickened or condensed. Centrioles are beginning to move apart and spindle fibers are forming between them.

   c. Mid prophase: The nuclear membrane is still visible. Centrioles have moved to opposite ends of the cell, and spindle fibers are formed.

   d. Late prophase: The nuclear membrane has disappeared. Centrioles are at opposite ends of the cell, and the spindle is well formed.

   e. Metaphase: Chromosomes are lined up on the equator of the cell.

   f. Early anaphase: Chromosomes are just beginning to separate and move away from their positions on the equator.

   g. Late anaphase: Chromosomes are completely separated.

h. Telophase: Chromosomes arrive at the poles of the cell.

i. Cytokinesis: The cytoplasm begins to pinch in the middle to form two cells.

4. Label the cells to indicate the phases of mitosis.

5. In each cell, label the chromosomes, centrioles, nuclear membrane, nucleolus, and spindle fibers.

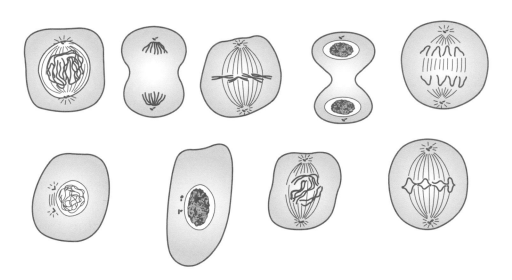

Figure 1

Stages of mitosis in random order

Procedure, Part B

1. Figure 2 shows a microscopic view of the cells in the tip of a growing onion root. Notice that some cells are in interphase and others are in various stages of mitosis.

2. Count the number of cells in each phase of mitosis. Copy the Data Table in your science notebook and record the counts.

3. Count the total number of cells in the figure. Record the number of cells in your science notebook.

4. Determine the percentage of cells in each phase of mitosis. To do so, divide the number of cells in each stage by the total number of cells in the view and multiply by 100. Record the answers in the column titled percentage.

5. Answer Analysis questions 4 through 7.

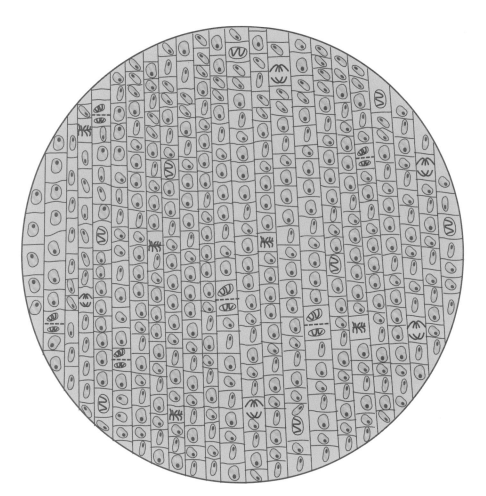

Figure 2

Onion root tip cells

Data Table		
Phase of mitosis	**Number of cells**	**Percentage**
Prophase		
Metaphase		
Anaphase		
Telophase		

Analysis

1. Describe the nucleus of an interphase cell.

2. Why do you think the nucleus of a prophase cell looks different from one in an interphase cell?

3. Describe the appearance of cells in metaphase, anaphase, and telophase.

4. What percentage of the cells in the root tip are in interphase?

5. Based on your findings, in what phase does a cell spend most of its life?

6. Why do you think we selected a root tip to look for mitotic cells?

7. Suggest some other tissues where cells might be undergoing mitosis.

What's Going On?

In actively growing tissue, some of the cells are undergoing mitosis. Even so, most cells are in interphase, the time between two mitotic divisions. During interphase, cells grow in size and synthesize new organelles. The cells' DNA is in the form of *chromatin*, long thin strands that are not clearly visible in the compound light microscope. However, one or more nucleoli can be seen. Each nucleolus holds genes for making ribosomal RNA (rRNA). During mitosis, these genes separate, but come back together in daughter cells. In interphase, the nuclear membrane is clearly visible.

Just before mitosis begins, the cell's DNA makes copies. At the same time, organelles also make copies so that each daughter cell will have everything it needs. In prophase, the DNA condenses or forms short coils. This shortening of the DNA makes it easier for the cell to maneuver the nuclear material. When mitosis is over and two daughter cells have been formed, the nuclear membrane reforms, the nucleoli reappear, and the chromatin relaxes into long strands once again.

Connections

Mitosis is a carefully controlled process that is regulated by several genes. However, *cancer* is a disease of mitosis in which cells do not respond to the normal regulators. Cancer can be caused by a mutation in a gene that regulates mitosis. For example, the gene p54 regulates the normal cell cycle. In many cancers, this gene is defective. Another example is the gene BRCA1, which prevents formation of tumors. If this gene undergoes mutations, breast cancer can result. In both of these genes, cells undergo mitosis without control, dividing indefinitely. Normally, cells only go through mitosis about 50 times before they die.

Rapidly dividing cells can form a tumor, a mass of cells. Tumors may be *benign* or *malignant*. A benign tumor does not spread to other sites in the body and can usually be removed surgically. Malignant tumors travel through the blood or lymph to other parts of the body, creating new tumors. Malignant tumors cannot always be removed by surgery. Other cancer treatments include *radiation therapy* and *chemotherapy*. In radiation therapy, high doses of radiation are focused on tumors to kill cancerous cells. The drugs used for chemotherapy treat cancer by preventing mitosis. Two of these drugs are derived from plants, paclitaxil and vincristine. Both prevent the formation of a mitotic spindle in dividing cells. Other drugs stop mitosis by either preventing DNA from unwinding for replication or by interfering with nucleotides forming base-pairs with an unwound strand of DNA in the process of replication.

Want to Know More?

See appendix for Our Findings.

Further Reading

"Mitosis," December 2007. Developmental Biology Online. Available online. URL: http://www.uoguelph.ca/zoology/devobio/210labs/mitosis1.html. Accessed November 23, 2009. This Web site shows beautiful photographs of whitefish blastula cells undergoing mitosis.

"Mystery Behind How Nuclear Membrane Forms During Mitosis Solved," September 21, 2007. ScienceDaily. Available online. URL: http://www.sciencedaily.com/releases/2007/09/070915100302.htm. Accessed November 24, 2009. By observing frog eggs, scientists at Salk Institute of Biological Sciences have shown that nuclear membranes in daughter cells are made from tubules of the endoplasmic reticulum.

"Types of Cancer," National Cancer Institute. Available online. URL: http://www.cancer.gov/. Accessed November 23, 2009. At this Web page, links provide information on several types of cancer and cancer treatments.

2. Amino Acids in Sickle Cell Anemia

Topic

A mutation in one nucleic acid in hemoglobin causes sickle cell anemia.

Introduction

Hemoglobin is a protein found in *erythrocytes*, red blood cells. This molecule is responsible for carrying oxygen from the lungs to cells in the body. Oxygen is used by cells to carry out *cellular respiration*, the process in which glucose is oxidized to make energy in the form of adenosine triphosphate or *ATP*. Each hemoglobin molecule is made up of four parts: two alpha chains and two beta chains. In sickle-cell anemia, the genes for the beta chains contain an error. As a result, the entire protein is deformed and takes on a stiff, sickle shape.

The abnormal protein is made by the same process used to make all proteins in cells. First, the *deoxyribonucleic acid* (*DNA*) double helix unzips, exposing a section of *nucleotides*. Then free *messenger RNA (mRNA)* nucleotides in the nucleus base pair with the exposed DNA nucleotides. In *ribonucleic acid (RNA)*, the nucleotide adenine binds to uracil (A-U) and cytosine to guanine (C-G). As these nucleotides assemble in the correct order, they form a chain. When the chain is complete, it leaves the nucleus and moves into the cytoplasm where it attaches to a *ribosome*, providing the information needed to code for a protein. Each *codon*, or set of three bases on mRNA, codes for a particular amino acid.

In this experiment, you will examine a portion of the DNA nucleotide that codes for normal hemoglobin and a section that codes for sickle cell hemoglobin to see how the abnormal protein is produced.

Time Required

45 minutes

Materials

- scissors
- tape
- photocopies of figures 1 through 3
- science notebook

Safety Note Take care when working with scissors. Please review and follow the safety guidelines at the beginning of this volume.

Procedure

1. Use scissors to cut out the shapes of a portion of the DNA strand for normal hemoglobin and a portion of the DNA strand for sickle-cell hemoglobin from the photocopy of Figure 1 on page 9. Answer Analysis question 1.

2. Use scissors to cut out the mRNA nucleotide shapes from the photocopy of Figure 2 on page 10, and the amino acids shapes from the photocopy of Figure 3 on page 11.

3. Place the strand of normal hemoglobin DNA on your desktop. Use the RNA base-pairing rules to construct a strand of mRNA from the mRNA nucleotide shapes using the DNA strand for normal hemoglobin as a template. Tape the mRNA bases together to keep the strand intact.

4. Use the data table on page 10 to determine the amino acids that are coded by the mRNA strand you just created. For example, if you have a codon that reads UUU, it codes for the amino acid phenylaline. Align the correct amino acid shapes along the strand of mRNA. Tape the shapes together at their connectors to make a short *polypeptide*.

5. Repeat steps 3 and 4 for the portion of the DNA strand for sickle-cell hemoglobin. Answer Analysis questions 2 through 4.

6. Compare the shapes of the two short strands of amino acids.

7. Answer Analysis questions 5 through 7.

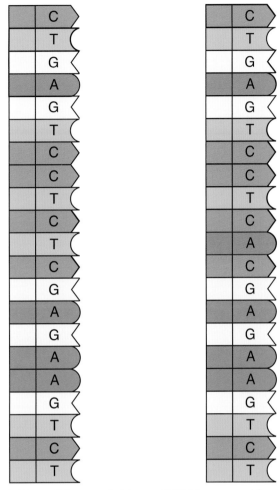

DNA in sickle-cell hemoglobin   DNA in normal hemoglobin

Figure 1

Analysis

1. How do the DNA strands for normal hemoglobin and sickle-cell hemoglobin differ?

2. How do the mRNA strands produced by these two hemoglobins differ?

3. How do the sequences of amino acids produced by these two hemoglobins differ?

4. How did the presence of glutamic acid affect the chain of amino acids?

5. Some amino acids have a charge (− or +) and some are neutral. Amino acids with charges are described as *polar*. Examine the structural formulas of glutamic acid and valine in Figure 4 on page 12. Which one has a charge?

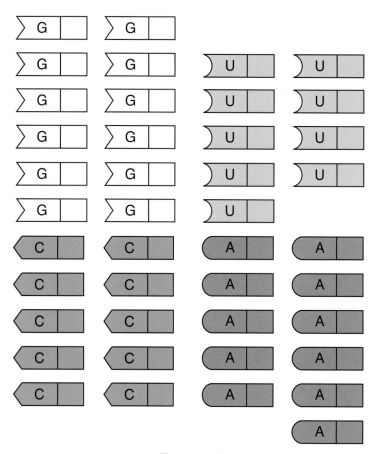

Figure 2
mRNA nucleotides

Data Table

	second letter				
first letter	**U**	**C**	**A**	**G**	
U	UUU UUC phenyl-alanine / UUA UUG leucine	UCU UCC UCA UCG serine	UAU UAC tyrosine / UAA stop codon UAG stop codon	UGU UGC cysteine / UGA stop codon / UGG tryptophan	U C A G
C	CUU CUC CUA CUG leucine	CCU CCC CCA CCG proline	CAU CAC histidine / CAA CAG glutamine	CGU CGC CGA CGG arginine	U C A G
A	AUU AUC isoleucine / AUA methionine: / AUG initiation codon	ACU ACC ACA ACG threonine	AAU AAC asparagine / AAA AAG lysine	AGU AGC serine / AGA AGG arginine	U C A G
G	GUU GUC GUA GUG valine	GCU GCC GCA GCG alanine	GAU GAC aspartic acid / GAA GAG glutamic acid	GGU GGC GGA GGG glycine	U C A G

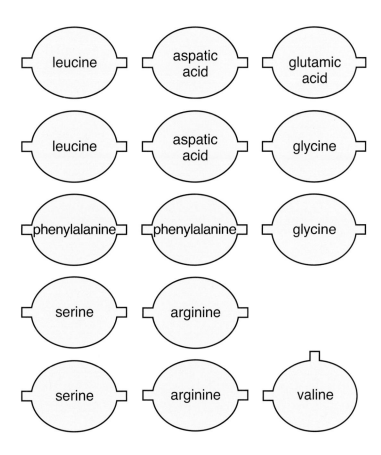

Figure 3

Amino acid shapes

6. What would you expect to happen if a negatively charged amino acid and a positively charged amino acid are close to each other?

7. Based on your answer to Analysis question 6, how can polar amino acids affect the shape of a protein?

What's Going On?

Sickle cell hemoglobin differs from normal hemoglobin by only one amino acid. The presence of valine in the amino acid chain affects the way the protein folds, giving the finished product the wrong shape. The incorrect folding of hemoglobin's beta chains causes hemoglobin molecules to stick together and clump, deforming the shape of the red blood cell that contains them. The body destroys these abnormal cells, leading to *anemia*. In addition, the misshapen cells clog capillaries, preventing the delivery of oxygen to tissues or organs and causing pain (see Figures 5a and 5b on pages 12 and 13).

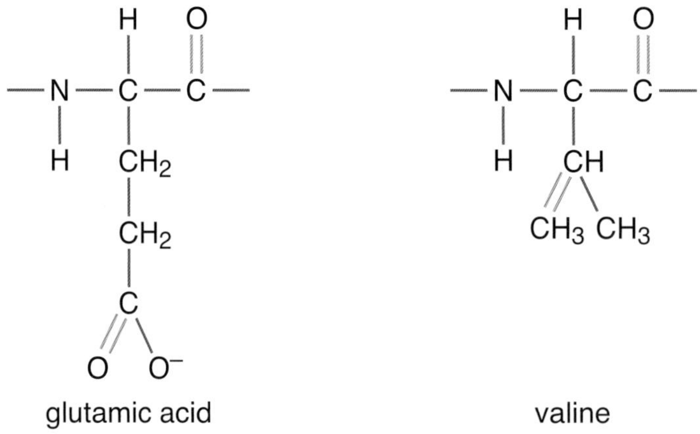

glutamic acid   valine

Figure 4

Connections

Anemia is any type of blood disease that results in an abnormally low red blood cell count. Red blood cells are made in the marrow of long bones. Normally, red blood cells circulate in the body for about 120 days. However, sickled red blood cells have a much shorter life, living only 10 to 20 days. The bone marrow is unable to replace the lost cells fast enough, so fewer red blood cells are in circulation to carry oxygen to cells.

Sickle cell anemia is a genetic disease caused by a recessive trait. To inherit the disease, an individual receives one recessive gene (S) from each parent, resulting in the genotype SS. If each parent carries one normal gene (A) and one sickle gene (S), each of their offspring have a 25 percent chance of inheriting the disease. The likelihood of inheriting the disease is shown in the *punnett square* in Figure 6 on page 13. In many cases, parents do not know that they carry the trait.

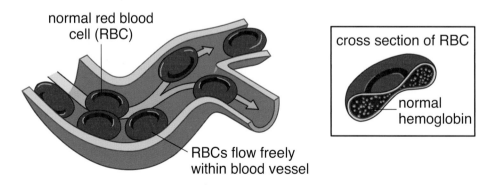

Figure 5a

Normal red blood cells

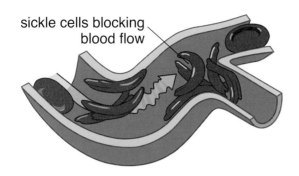
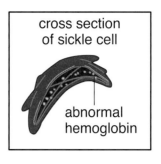

Figure 5b

Abnormal, sickled, red blood cells (sickle cells)

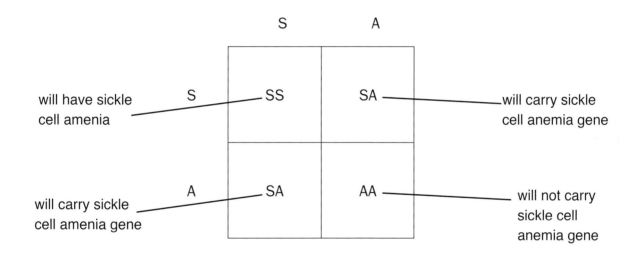

will have sickle cell amenia — S — SS

will carry sickle cell amenia gene — A — SA

SA — will carry sickle cell anemia gene

AA — will not carry sickle cell anemia gene

Figure 6

Parents who carry the gene for sickle cell anemia have the genotype SA. Two parents with this genotype can pass the trait to their offspring. This Punnett square shows that their offspring have 25 percent chance of inheriting the disease.

Want to Know More?

See appendix for Our Findings.

Further Reading

Bender, M. A., and William Hobbs. "Sickle Cell Disease," September 17, 2009. *Gene Reviews*. Available online. URL: http://www.ncbi.nlm.nih.gov/bookshelf/br.fcgi?book=gene&part=sickle#sickle.Summary. Accessed November 29, 2009. In this advanced article, Bender and Hobbs explain the causes, symptoms, and treatments for this disease.

"Sickle Cell Anemia," 2007. Genes and Disease. Available online. URL: http://www.ncbi.nlm.nih.gov/bookshelf/br.fcgi?book=gnd&part=anemia sicklecell. Accessed March 31, 2010. This Web site provides a concise description of the disease and explains why hydroxyurea, an antitumor drug, is useful in treatment.

"Sickle Cell Disease," November 20, 2009. *Genetics Home Reference*. Available online. URL: http://ghr.nlm.nih.gov. Accessed March 31, 2010. Information on the inheritance of sickle cell anemia as well as disease symptoms and their causes are described on this Web site.

3. Genetic Engineering With Plasmids

Topic

The steps in transferring genes to plasmids can be demonstrated with models.

Introduction

Bacteria are *prokaryotes*, cells that lack nuclei and organelles. The DNA of bacteria is not contained in chromosomes like those found in human cells. Instead, these cells have long strands of DNA floating in the cytoplasm, the jelly like material inside the cell'smembrane. In addition, bacterial cells have small loops of DNA called *plasmid*s. Plasmids are tiny and only carry a few genes. Some plasmids carry genes that make cells resistant to antibiotics.

Biologists have found that plasmids can be used in *gene cloning*, a type of genetic engineering. In this procedure, a gene of interest, such as the gene that codes for insulin, is identified and copied. The basic steps are:

1. The gene of interest is located and removed from human DNA using *restriction enzymes*, enzymes that cut DNA at particular sequences (Figure 1).
2. Bacterial plasmids are isolated and cut open with the same restriction enzyme.
3. The plasmids and genes of interest are mixed. Some genes and plasmids combine, producing *recombinant DNA* (Figure 2).
4. The recombinant DNA is placed in bacterial cells. Not all bacteria take up the plasmids.
5. The bacteria are grown on petri dishes containing growth medium and an antibiotic. Only the cells that took up the plasmids are antibiotic resistant and able to survive. These cells also contain the gene of interest.
6. The bacteria are grown in large quantities. They produce insulin, which is removed and used to make medication.

In this experiment, you will use a model to recreate these steps.

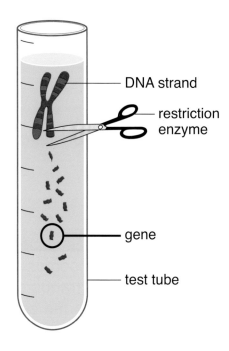

Figure 1

Restriction enzyme in the test tube cuts off a portion of the DNA strand.

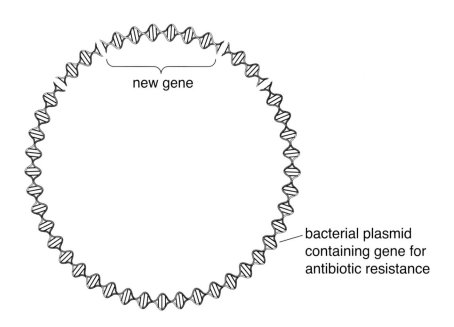

Figure 2

Recombinant plasmid

Time Required

45 minutes

Materials

- ◌◦ strip of white paper about 6 inches (in.) (15.2 centimeters [cm] x 2 in. [5 cm]) long
- ◌◦ strip of colored paper about 6 in. (15.2 cm) x 2 in. (5 cm) long
- ◌◦ scissors
- ◌◦ tape
- ◌◦ highlighter pen
- ◌◦ science notebook

Safety Note Take care when working with scissors. Please review and follow the safety guidelines at the beginning of this volume.

Procedure

1. The following sequence represents one strand of DNA found in a plasmid. The gene for antibiotic resistance is underlined. Copy the sequence onto a strip of colored paper.

   A T A T C A A G C T T C C C G A G A C T T A C C C C A G A <u>G A C A C G</u> A A A

2. Tape the two free ends of the strip of paper together to make a circle. The paper circle represents a plasmid.

3. To open a plasmid ring, a biologist uses a restriction enzyme. One such enzyme is HindIII, which cuts DNA between two adenines (As) in the sequence A A G C T T. To simulate the opening of the plasmid DNA with HindIII, find the sequence A A G C T T. Use scissors to cut between the two As. The scissors represent a restriction enzyme.

4. The next step is to insert a human gene. A section of nucleotides that represents human DNA appears on the top of page 18. This DNA includes the gene for insulin: C C C T A G A A C A A. Copy the

entire sequence onto a strip of white paper.

A A G C T T A A A A T A G C A T C C C T A G A A C A A C C C A A G C T T

5. Highlight the gene for insulin.

6. Look for the sequence A A G C T T before the gene for insulin. When you find the sequence, use the scissors to cut between the two As, simulating the use of HindIII to cut out the gene. Discard the short section of DNA that is not attached to the insulin gene.

7. Look for the same sequence after the gene for insulin. When you find the sequence, use scissors to cut between the two As. Discard the short section of DNA that is not attached to the insulin gene. (After cutting, the insulin gene may have some extra nucleotides attached to it, which is fine.)

8. Tape the section of DNA that you cut out of white paper, which includes the gene for insulin, inside the plasmid.

Analysis

1. In this experiment, what do the scissors represent?

2. In this experiment, what does the tape represent?

3. When you simulated the use of HindIII to cut open the plasmid, did you cut into the gene for antibiotic resistance?

4. Why is it important in genetic engineering that the plasmid retain the gene for antibiotic resistance?

5. Which of the following represents recombinant DNA:

   a. the strip of white paper with the gene for insulin

   b. the strip of colored paper with the plasmid DNA

   c. the strip of white paper taped into the colored paper?

   Explain your reasoning.

6. Why do you think that bacteria are able to translate a human gene into a protein?

7. Suggest some other uses for recombinant DNA.

What's Going On?

HindIII is just one of several restriction enzymes. In this simulation, you used HindIII because it is able to cut a DNA sequence that was found in the plasmid DNA as well as on both ends of the insulin DNA. Using the scissors to represent HindIII, you cut open the plasmid, and then cut out the gene for insulin. By taping the two pieces of paper together, you simulated the creation a piece of recombinant DNA. In a genetic laboratory, the next step would be to mix the recombinant plasmids with bacteria so that the bacteria would take up the plasmids. The uptake is not 100 percent, so bacteria that do take up the plasmid must be separated. This is where the gene for antibiotic resistance becomes important. The bacteria are grown on petri dishes of nutrients that contain an antibiotic. Only the bacteria that have taken up the plasmid survive.

Connections

Geneticists must take into account the fact that DNA is a double-stranded molecule. When restriction enzymes are used, they actually cut through both strands. Some restriction enzyme cuts are not straight across. Instead, the staggered cuts produce single-stranded ends that can easily bond to DNA fragments cut with the same enzymes. These are known as "sticky ends" (see Figure 3).

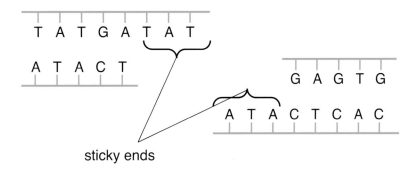

Figure 3

When the sticky end of a plasmid and the complementary sticky end of a DNA sequence meet, the nucleotides in each are attracted to each other by *hydrogen bonds*. Hydrogen bonds are not strong. To hold the two pieces together permanently, *covalent bonds* must form along the sugar-phosphate backbone of the strands. These bonds are catalyzed by enzymes known as *ligases*. The process of forming covalent bonds along the backbone of DNA or RNA strands is known as *ligation*.

Want to Know More?

See appendix for Our Findings.

Further Reading

"Genetic Engineering," 2009. *Science Clarified*. Available online. URL: http://www.scienceclarified.com/scitech/Genetics/Genetic-Engineering. html. Accessed November 29, 2009. This Web site reviews the history of genetic engineering and discusses the use of plasmids.

Hain, Patty, and James Ehly. "Gene Cloning," 2000. Available online. URL: http://citnews.unl.edu/hscroptechnology/html/animationOut.cgi?anim_ name=genecloning.swf. Accessed November 29, 2009. This animation on genetic engineering with plasmids is provided by the University of Nebraska.

Johnson, George. "Here Is How Genetic Engineering Is Done," *On Science,* 2008. Available online. URL: http://txtwriter.com/onscience/Articles/ geneEng.html. Accessed June 16, 2010. Dr. Johnson is a science teacher who discusses current science issues in his weekly "On Science" column in the St. Louis *Beacon*. In this column, he explains genetic engineering in plants.

4. Meiosis

Topic

Spermatogenesis and oogenesis are both meiotic divisions, but with some important differences.

Introduction

Meiosis is the series of cell divisions in which *diploid* cells in the reproductive organs develop into *haploid gametes*. Because meiosis reduces the number of chromosomes by one half, it is also known as reduction division. The time frame of meiotic events in males and females shows differences. Females produce one egg cell a month from *puberty* to *menopause*. Males produce hundreds of thousands of sperm daily from puberty until old age.

Each human cell contains 46 chromosomes, or 23 pairs. One pair was inherited from the mother and a similar set was inherited from the father. Matching pairs of chromosomes are similar in size and are known as *homologs*.

The events of reduction division are divided in stages labeled *meiosis I* and *meiosis II*. In each stage, the following steps occur: prophase, metaphase, anaphase, telophase, and cytokinesis. Prophase I is one of the most complex periods. In prophase 1, matching or homologous sets of sister chromatids come together. As a result, four sister chromatids are physically joined for a short time, forming a *tetrad*. In this time, the chromatids overlap or cross over, and pieces of DNA are swapped. In metaphase I, the tetrads are lined up on the cell's equator. During anaphase I, the tetrads are pulled apart so that each set of homologous sister chromatids moves to opposite ends of the cell. The chromatids reach the opposite poles in telophase I and the cytoplasm pinches in half in cytokinesis to form two cells.

Each of the resulting cells undergoes meiosis II, which is similar to *mitosis*. In this stage, the chromosomes in each cell prepare to divide again in prophase II. During metaphase II, they are lined up on the equator. The sister chromatids are pulled toward opposite poles in anaphase II. During telophase II and cytokinesis, they reach the poles and the cytoplasm is pinched in half to form two cells.

Although the basic process in males and females is the same, there are some important differences. In this experiment, you will create a model of *oogenesis*, gamete production in females, and *spermatogenesis*, gamete production in males.

Time Required

55 minutes

Materials

- clay or Play-Doh™ of 2 colors
- long sheet of stiff construction paper or cardboard
- science notebook

Safety Note   Please review and follow the safety guidelines at the beginning of this volume.

Procedure

1. Create a display that shows the steps of meiosis in an egg cell that contains two pairs of homologous chromosomes. To do so:

   a. Tape together two pieces of stiff construction paper or cut out a long piece of cardboard.

   b. At one end of the paper, draw a circle that represents a female diploid cell, the *oogonium*. This is the cell that will produce an egg. Place two pieces of clay of one color, each about the size of your little finger, in the cell to represent a chromosome that has already replicated. Pinch these two pieces together at the center. Place two pieces of clay of another color in the cell to represent another chromosome that has replicated. Also pinch these chromosomes together. All four pieces of clay should be the same size. In this cell model, you are showing two homologous chromosomes, one from each parent, that have replicated to form their sister chromatids.

   c. The first stage of meiosis is prophase I. In this stage, homologous chromosomes undergo *synapsis*, or crossing over. Draw another circle to show the events of prophase 1 in oogenesis. Put two more sets of chromosomes in this circle, just like the first ones, but join them together to form a tetrad.

d. Pinch off a section of each chromosome. Swap the sections as shown in Figure 1.

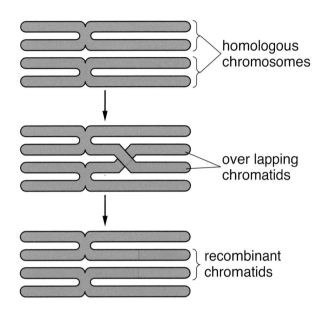

Figure 1

Sister chromatids cross over and exchange pieces of DNA.

e. In the next stage, metaphase I, the tetrads line up on the cell's equator. In this example, you have one tetrad. Draw another circle and prepare pieces of clay to represent this tetrad. Do not forget to show the chromosomes that have swapped pieces of DNA. Arrange the tetrad at the equator.

f. In anaphase I, tetrads are pulled apart so that each homologous pair moves toward opposite poles of the cells. Demonstrate this by separating the tetrad, keeping the sister chromatids together.

g. In telophase I, the sister chromatids reach the poles of the cell and the cell divides in two. In oogenesis, one of the cells is large and the other is very small. To show these events, draw two circles, one about the same size as the earlier circles and one much smaller. Create more clay chromosomes so that you can show one set of sister chromatids in the big circle and one in the small circle. Label the large circle as the *oocyte* and the small circle as the *polar body.*

h. Meiosis II occurs in the regular cell and in the polar body. In prophase II, each cell prepares to divide again. You will not show this stage in your model because it looks very similar to telophase II.

i. In metaphase II, the chromosomes line up on the equator. Beside the oocyte, draw a large circle and a small circle. Beside the polar body, draw two small circles. In each cell, put a set of sister chromatids on the equator.

j. In anaphase II, the sister chromatids are pulled apart and move to the opposite ends of the cell. Show these events with circles and clay.

k. In telophase II, the sister chromatids reach the ends of the cells and the cells undergo cytokinesis, producing two new cells. Using Figure 2 as a model, show this last step in the event with circles and clay or Play-Doh™.

2. Answer Analysis questions 1 through 4.

3. Using a different piece of stiff paper or cardboard and clay or Play-Doh™, create a similar display showing the stages of *spermatogenesis*. Label each stage, beginning with prophase I and ending with telophase II. Refer to Figure 2. Notice that spermatogenesis follows the steps described in the Introduction and there are no polar bodies.

4. Answer Analysis questions 5 through 9.

Analysis

1. How many normal-size, functional cells were produced by oogenesis?

2. How many chromosomes were in the first cell of oogenesis?

3. How many chromosomes were in the last cells of oogenesis?

4. Were all chromosomes in the last cells the same? Why or why not?

5. How many normal-size, functional cells were produced by spermatogenesis?

6. How many chromosomes were in the first cell of spermatogenesis?

7. How many chromosomes were in the last cells of spermatogenesis?

8. Were all chromosomes in the last cells the same? Why or why not?

9. What event in meiosis produces genetic variation in offspring?

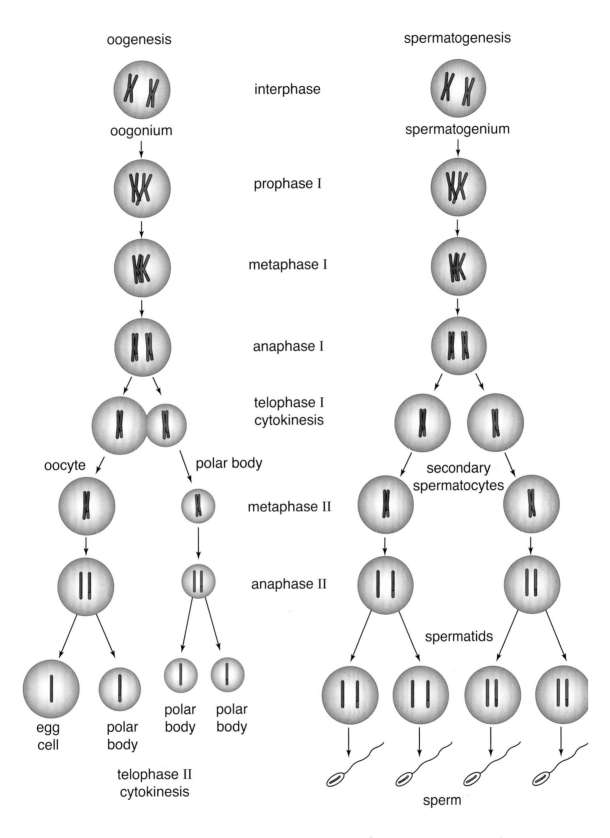

Figure 2

Stages of meiosis

What's Going On?

Meiosis produces haploid cells for reproduction. The eggs and sperm that result from meiosis only contain one-half of the normal complement of chromosomes. When a sperm and egg fuse in the process of *fertilization*, the full diploid number is restored.

In males, the four cells that are produced are spermatids, which undergo further changes to develop into mature, *motile* sperm. In females, only one cell that will develop into a mature egg is produced. The other, smaller cells are polar bodies and they disintegrate. The unequal division is due to the fact that the developing oocyte receives most of the cytoplasm as well as the organelles, mRNAs, and enzymes during division. This assures that the egg cell will have all the supplies it needs for the *zygote*.

Connections

Fertilization usually takes place in the *oviducts,* tubes that connect the ovaries to the uterus. When an egg cell is fertilized, it has not yet completed meiosis II. Penetration by the sperm stimulates the cell to finish meiosis II, producing the ovum and the second polar body. The chromosomes of the egg and sperm fuse, producing a diploid nucleus in the zygote. Soon after fertilization, the zygote begins to undergo mitosis to form two diploid cells. This is the beginning of a series of divisions known as *cleavage*, the start of the development of the embryo. As the egg is undergoing cleavage, it completes its trip down the oviduct to the uterus, where it implants in the uterine wall. Here it will develop a *placenta* that enables the mother to supply nutrients and oxygen to the developing fetus.

 ## Want to Know More?

See appendix for Our Findings.

Further Reading

Ackerley, Sandra K. "Developmental Biology Online," June 29, 2009. Available online. URL: http://www.uoguelph.ca/zoology/devobio/dbindex. htm. Accessed November 29, 2009. This Web site from the University of Guelph, Ontario, Canada, provides detailed information on the processes of gamete production and development.

"DNA From the Beginning," 2002. Cold Springs Harbor Laboratory. Available online. URL: http://www.dnaftb.org/dnaftb/. Accessed November 29, 2009. This Web site provides animated tutorials on DNA and genetics.

O'Neill, Dennis. "Cell Reproduction," 2010. *The Biological Basis of Heredity: An Introduction to Basic Cell Structures Related to Genetic Inheritance*. Available online. URL: http://anthro.palomar.edu/biobasis/ bio_2.htm. Accessed February 9, 2010. O'Neill of Palomar College, San Marcos, California, created and maintains Biological Basis of Heredity, a site that provides information on topics such as cell structures, recombination, and gene linkage. This particular page gives clear explanations of mitosis and meiosis.

5. Inheritance of Traits

Topic
Dominant and recessive traits create predictable patterns of inheritance.

Introduction
Gregor Mendel (1822–84) experimented with pea plants to find out how traits are passed from parent to offspring. He determined that the traits in peas had two units or "factors" of inheritance, one from each parent. Scientists now know that many traits have two forms or *alleles* of a gene.

Although most traits in humans are determined by multiple genes, some are inherited from only two alleles of a gene. One allele is provided by the mother and the other by the father. The two inherited alleles can be both *dominant*, both *recessive*, or hybrid, a combination of each. In a hybrid, the dominant trait is always expressed and masks the presence of a recessive trait.

The genes of an organism are known as its *genotype*. The way an organism appears is its *phenotype*. Mendel found that if a pea plant inherited two dominant alleles for tallness, with the genotype TT, the plant's phenotype would be tall. The same was true if the plant inherited one dominant gene and one recessive gene with the genotype Tt. Short plants, which have inherited two recessive genes, have the genotype tt. In this experiment, you will simulate the inheritance of dominant and recessive traits in humans.

Time Required
45 minutes

Materials

- 2 coins
- 1 sheet of plain white paper
- colored pencils
- science notebook

Safety Note   Please review and follow the safety procedures at the beginning of this volume.

Procedure

1. In this experiment, you will work with a partner to create a fictitious offspring. Designate one partner as the father and the other as the mother.

2. Each partner needs a coin, which will be used to determine whether that partner is contributing the dominant or recessive allele of a trait to a fictitious offspring. If a coin flip yields heads, you contribute a dominant allele. If the flip is tails, you contribute a recessive allele.

3. Answer Analysis questions 1 through 3.

4. Copy the data table in your science notebook. As you do, examine the list of traits found in humans. The first trait listed is face shape. To show that both parents contribute an allele to the shape of their offspring's face, both you and your partner should flip coins. After flipping, write the alleles that each of you flipped in the correct column. (If you flipped heads, you provide the allele O; if your partner flipped tails, he or she has the allele o.

5. Write the combination of alleles in the column labeled "Baby's Genotype."

6. If the genotype is OO or Oo, the baby's phenotype is "oval face." If the genotype is oo, the face is square. Write the baby's phenotype in the last column.

7. Repeat steps 4 through 6 for the traits listed below. In each case, record the genotype and the phenotype.

   a. SS or Ss is a smooth chin with no cleft. A cleft chin (Figure 1) is ss.

   b. CC is curly hair, Cc is wavy hair, and cc is straight hair.

   c. WW and Ww are a widow's peak at the hairline. A straight hairline is ww (Figure 2).

   d. Almond-shaped eyes are dominant, AA or Aa. Round eyes, aa, are recessive.

   e. Free earlobes (Figure 3) are dominant, FF or Ff. Attached earlobes are recessive, ff.

   f. Freckles are dominant, FF or Ff. Lack of freckles is recessive, ff.

Figure 1

A cleft chin is due to the inheritance of two recessive alleles.

Figure 2

A widow's peak is due to a dominant trait.

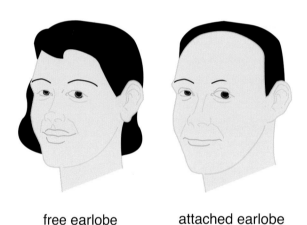

free earlobe   attached earlobe

Figure 3

Free earlobes are due to a dominant trait.

> g. Long eyelashes, LL or Ll, are dominant to short eyelashes, ll.
>
> h. Dimples are dominant, DD or Dd, to no dimples, dd.
>
> i. Separated eyebrows, SS or Ss, are dominant to joined eyebrows, ss.
>
> j. Dark hair, DD or Dd, is dominant over light-colored hair, dd.
>
> k. Brown eyes, BB or Bb, are dominant over blue eyes, bb.

8. When the data table is complete, draw the face of the baby showing all of its traits.

9. Answer Analysis questions 4 through 7.

Data Table				
Trait	Mother's allele	Father's allele	Baby's genotype	Baby's phenotype
Face shape				
Smooth or cleft chin				
Curly, wavy, or straight hair				
Widow's peak or straight hairline				
Eye shape				
Earlobes				
Freckles				
Eyelashes				
Dimples				
Eyebrows				
Hair color				
Eye color				

Analysis

1. If you flip a coin once, what is the likelihood that you will flip heads? If you continue to flip the coin until you have completed 99 flips, what is the likelihood that the 100th flip will be heads?

2. If a trait has only two alleles, dominant and recessive, what is the likelihood that a parent will pass on the dominant trait?

3. How many recessive alleles must an offspring inherit to show the recessive phenotype?

4. If you and your partner repeated this activity, would you expect your second offspring to look just like the first? Explain your answer.

5. In this experiment, what is unique about the inheritance of curls?

6. Explain why two brothers in a family may look very different.

7. Both of the parents of a child have brown eyes and the child has brown eyes. Would it be possible for the next child in the family to have blue eyes? Explain your answer.

What's Going On?

Many genetic traits are controlled by genes that have only two alleles: dominant and recessive. By flipping coins, you and your partner simulated the inheritance of genes. The characteristics of your fictitious offspring were due to chance. If you and your partner had decided to have two more offspring, they would have had some of the same traits as the first, but there would be some differences.

Not all genes follow Mendel's law of dominance. Some traits show *incomplete dominance*, and neither trait is dominant over the other. Instead, the traits blend to produce an intermediate form. In this lab, wavy hair is an intermediate form between straight and curly due in incomplete dominance. Other traits show *codominance* in which both dominant traits are expressed. Blood type is a trait that shows codominance. The genes A and B are two alleles for blood type that are codominant and produce the blood type AB.

Connections

Many genetic diseases are caused by *mutations* in single genes and show mendelian dominance. In these conditions, the mutated gene causes the protein to be assembled incorrectly, resulting in a protein that cannot carry out its job. More than 6,000 single gene disorders have been identified. Included in this group are sickle cell anemia, cystic fibrosis, marfan syndrome, and Huntington's disease. Sickle cell anemia is a blood disorder in which some of the red blood cells take on a spiky shape which prevents them from carrying oxygen to cells. In cystic fibrosis, the body produces thick, sticky mucus in the lungs and digestive tract, interfering with normal growth and development. Marfan syndrome is a disorder of connective tissue, which is found throughout the body in cartilage, tendons, ligaments, heart valves, and other structures. People who inherit Huntington's disease suffer loss of nerve cells in the brain, which can lead to uncontrolled movements, loss of speech, and antisocial behavior.

Want to Know More?

See appendix for Our Findings.

Further Reading

"Genetic Disorder Information on the Web," May 23, 2003. Available online. URL: http://www.ornl.gov/sci/techresources/Human_Genome/ posters/chromosome/diseaseindex.shtml. Accessed November 29, 2009. This extensive Web site explains genetic diseases, discusses their inheritance, symptoms, and treatment, and provides links to other sites.

McClean, Phillip. "Mendelian Genetics," 2000. Available online. URL: http://www.ndsu.edu/pubweb/~mcclean/plsc431/mendel/mendel1.htm. Accessed November 30, 2009. McClean simply explains how dominant and recessive traits are passed on to successive generations.

"Mendelian Genetics." The Biology Project. Available online. URL: http:// www.biology.arizona.edu/mendelian_genetics/mendelian_genetics.html. Accessed November 30, 2009. This tutorial Web site focuses on several topics, including monohybrid crosses.

6. Predicted and Actual Results of Genetic Crosses

Topic

Punnett squares are useful in predicting the results of genetic crosses.

Introduction

Before the work of the pioneer Austrian geneticist Gregor Mendel (1822–84), scientists believed that the traits of parents blended to produce the traits seen in offspring. Mendel disproved this concept, using a strict experimental procedure in which he gathered the results of many genetic crosses. In his experiments, Mendel began with pure-breeding organisms, those that always produced offspring like themselves. By mating two different pure-breeders, he produced *hybrids*, which have traits from each parent. Mendel found that some traits are *dominant* and have the ability to mask *recessive traits*.

The experiments conducted by Mendel involved hundreds of pea plants. After crossing plants and observing, counting, and recording the appearance of their offspring over a period of several years, he concluded that the *F1 generation*, the first generation of offspring, resembles only one of the parents. In the *F2 generation*, the result of mating F1 organisms, 75 percent of the offspring looked like the F1 organisms, but the characteristic of the other original parent showed up about 25 percent of the time. In other words, in the F2 generation, the ratio of one trait to the other was 3:1. Mendel explained that traits appeared as they did because one was dominant and the other recessive. Figure 1 shows how the dominant trait for tallness masked the recessive trait for shortness in the F1 generation of pea plants. Shortness appeared again in the F2 generation.

Mendel believed that the traits were passed down from parents to offspring as "factors." Today, scientists know that these factors are *genes,* segments of DNA that code for particular traits. Genes can have two or more forms or *alleles*. A dominant allele can prevent the appearance of a recessive one. Geneticists refer to the actual genes of an offspring as the *genotype*; the appearance of an offspring is its *phenotype*.

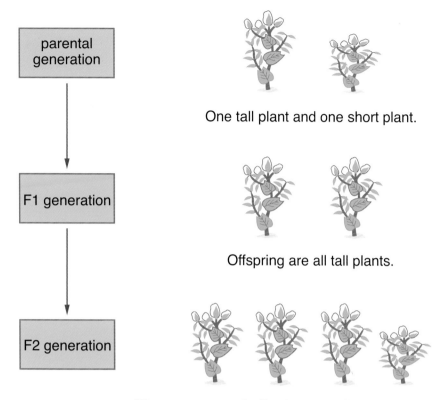

One tall plant and one short plant.

Offspring are all tall plants.

Three-quarters of offspring are tall; one-quarter is short.

Figure 1

Using the data provided by Mendel, geneticists can use a Punnett square to predict the offspring of genetic crosses. The square is divided into four parts. One parent's alleles are written across the top of the square and the other parent's alleles along the side (see Figure 2). Every possible combination of genes is shown in the four sections. Animal breeders, farmers, geneticists, and many others find that the Punnett square can help predict the likelihood that any one offspring will inherit a specific set of alleles. In this experiment, you will use a Punnett square to predict the offspring of a cross between two guinea pigs, then you will simulate the cross to see if the predicted results are accurate.

Time Required

45 minutes

father's alleles

	D	d
d	Dd	dd
d	Dd	dd

mother's alleles

Figure 2

This Punnett square shows the cross between a father whose alleles are Dd and a mother with the alleles dd.

Materials

- ➥ 2 small paper bags
- ➥ 2 black pipe cleaners
- ➥ 2 white pipe cleaners
- ➥ science notebook

Safety Note Please review and follow the safety procedures at the beginning of this volume.

Procedure

1. In your science notebook, draw a Punnett square to show the expected results in the cross of two black guinea pigs with the genotypes Bb (see Figure 3). To do so, draw a box and divide it into sections. Write one parent's genotype, Bb, across the top of the box. Write the other parent's genotype, Bb, on the left side of the box. Write the possible combination of genes in the four sections.

2. Answer Analysis questions 1 through 3.

3. Find out how the expected results shown in the Punnett square compare to actual results of crossing the guinea pigs in a

simulation. Black pipe cleaners will represent the allele B; white pipe cleaners the allele b. To show the female guinea pig's alleles Bb, place a black pipe cleaner and a white pipe cleaner in one bag. Label the bag "Female." To show the male guinea pig's genes Bb, place another black pipe cleaner and another white pipe cleaner in a second bag. Label the bag "Male."

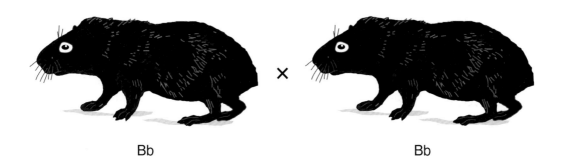

Bb   Bb

Figure 3

Both the male and female guinea pigs have the genotype Bb.

4. To simulate the mating of these two guinea pigs, shake the bags to mix the genes. Without looking, reach into each bag and pull out one pipe cleaner. These two pipe cleaners represent the genes of the first offspring. Record the genotype of the first offspring on the data table. Return the pipe cleaners to the bags.

5. Repeat step 4 nine more times.

6. Find the percentage of offspring with the BB genotype. To do so, divide the number of BB offspring by 10, the total number of offspring. Multiply the result by 100 by find percentage.

7. Repeat step 6 to find the percentage of Bb offspring and the percentage of bb offspring.

8. Answer Analysis question 4.

9. In your science notebook, create a data table similar to the one above, but include space for 100 offspring.

10. Repeat steps 4 through 7 for a total of 100 offspring. Answer Analysis question 5.

Data Table	
Offspring	**Genotype**
1	
2	
3	
4	
5	
6	
7	
8	
9	
10	

Analysis

1. What is the purpose of a Punnett square?

2. What percentage of the offspring of guinea pigs of this cross would you expect to have the following genotypes: a. BB; b. Bb; c. bb.

3. If this pair of guinea had 10 offspring, how many of them would you expect to have the genotypes: a. BB; b. Bb; c. bb.

4. How did the actual number of offsprings' genotypes in the simulation compare to the predicted number based on the Punnett square?

5. How did the actual number of each genotypes of offspring produced in the pipe cleaner simulation of 100 offspring compare to the predicted number based on the Punnett square?

What's Going On?

If you flip a coin 10 times, how many times would you expect to get heads? You might think that 50 percent of the flips would be heads and 50 percent tails. However, when you flip the coin, you could get three heads and seven tails or nine heads and one tails. If you flipped the coin 100 times, your results would be different. After 100 flips, about half of the results would be heads and the other half tails. In other words, the greater the experimental size, the more likely it is to reflect the expected results. Mendel understood this concept and collected the results of thousands of genetic crosses in his research.

In genetics, chance or *probability* plays a role. Organisms are *diploid*, meaning that they have two of each chromosome. One of these chromosomes was inherited from the organism's mother and the other from the father. Therefore, genetic traits carried on these chromosomes are influenced by both copies. In sexual reproduction, these two copies are randomly sorted into different eggs and sperm. During fertilization, when an egg and sperm fuse, chance determines which two traits will combine.

Connections

Two rules help explain what happens when probability plays a role. The *rule of independent events* tells us that events in the past have no effect on those in the future. For example, if you flipped a coin three times and got heads on each flip, the chance that your fourth flip would be heads is still only 50 percent. Another way of stating this is the chance of heads is always one-half because a coin has two sides.

The *rule of multiplication* looks at how different events affect each other. According to this rule, the chance that two events will happen together is equal to the product of the probabilities of each event. So if you were flipping two coins instead of one, the chance that you would flip two heads is one-half multiplied by one-half, or one-fourth. Both of the rules can be applied to the chance of inheriting genetic traits.

Want to Know More?

See appendix for Our Findings.

Further Reading

McClean, Phillip. "Mendelian Genetics," 2000. Available online. URL: http://www.ndsu.edu/pubweb/~mcclean/plsc431/mendel/mendel1.htm. Accessed November 30, 2009. McClean explains in simple language how dominant and recessive traits are passed on to successive generations.

"Monohybrid Cross Problem Set," 2004. The Biology Project, University of Arizona. Available online. URL: http://www.biology.arizona.edu/ Mendelian_Genetics/problem_sets/monohybrid_Cross/01t.html. Accessed December 12, 2009. This tutorial Web site provides examples of monohybrid crosses.

Tissot, Robert. "Mendelian Inheritance." Available online. URL: http:// www.uic.edu/classes/bms/bms655/lesson3.html. Accessed December 12, 2009. Tissot explains punnett squares, pedigrees, and the rules of inheritance related to dominant and recessive traits.

7. Inheritance of Taste

Topic

A person's ability to taste PTC paper is inherited.

Introduction

In 1931, Arthur Fox, an American chemist, was working with the chemical phenylthiocarbamide (PTC) in the powder form. Fox was transferring the powder from one container to another, and some of the dust became airborne. His colleague complained about the bitter taste of the dust, but Fox could not taste it. After surveying friends and family, Fox found that some people could taste PTC, while others could not. The ability to taste the powder seemed to run in families. He also learned that some tasters found the chemical to be intensely bitter, while others reported the flavor as mild.

In 2003, geneticists identified the single gene that codes for a receptor on the tongue that can detect PTC. The gene has four forms or *alleles*. One allele is nontasting; the other three are different forms of tasting. Each of these alleles codes for a protein that regulates the shape of the taste receptor, which establishes how well PTC can bind to the receptor (see Figure 1). Everyone inherits two alleles of the gene, one from each parent. In this experiment, you will design a procedure to learn more about the ability to taste PTC.

Time Required

10 minutes for part A
55 minutes for part B

Materials

- PTC test strips
- control test strips

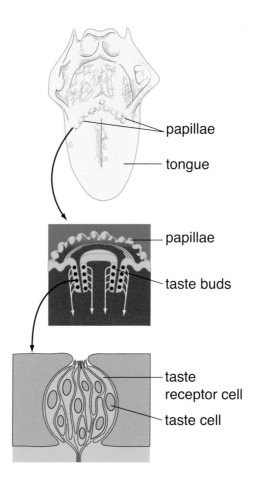

Figure 1

- ☞ small paper cup of water
- ☞ science notebook

Safety Note Please review and follow the safety precautions at the beginning of this volume.

Procedure, Part A

1. Take a sip of water from the paper cup and use it to rinse your mouth.

2. Taste the control strip. In your science notebook, describe how it tastes.

3. Taste the strip of PTC paper. In your science notebook, describe how it tastes.

4. Interview three classmates to see how your results compare to theirs.

Procedure, Part B

1. Design an experiment to answer one of the following questions:
    a. Is the ability to taste PTC dominant or recessive?
    b. What percentage of the school population is able to taste PTC?
    c. Is the ability to taste PTC more prevalent in males or females?
    d. Is there a correlation between the ability to taste PTC and the preference for foods in the mustard family (broccoli, cauliflower, and cabbage).

2. You can supplement the supplies provided by your teacher.

3. Before you conduct your experiment, decide exactly what you are going to do. Write the steps you plan to take (your experimental procedure) and the materials you plan to use (materials list) on the data table. Show your procedure and materials list to the teacher to find out if the procedure is acceptable and if the materials you want to use are available. If so, proceed with your experiment; if not, modify your work and show it to your teacher again.

4. Answer Analysis questions 1 through 3.

5. Once you have teacher approval, assemble the materials you need and begin your procedure.

6. Collect your results on a data table of your own design.

7. Answer Analysis questions 4 through 6.

Analysis

1. What is PTC paper?
2. Why are some people able to taste PTC paper while others are not?
3. Why does Part A of the Procedure ask you to taste the control strip?
4. What is your hypothesis?
5. Did you experiment support your hypothesis? Explain your reasoning.
6. If you could repeat this experiment, how would you improve it?

Data Table	
Your experimental procedure	
Your materials list	
Teacher's approval	

What's Going On?

Humans have the ability to detect a wide range of tastes, all of which can be grouped into four basic categories: bitter, sweet, salty, and sour. Taste buds for each type of taste are grouped in different regions of the tongue (see Figure 2). These tastes can be subdivided into hundreds of nuances of flavor. Geneticists have learned that the ability to detect certain tastes is controlled by DNA. The gene that detects the bitter taste of PTC is located on chromosome 7. This gene has 1,002 *nucleic acids* and differs from the nontaster gene by only three nucleic acids.

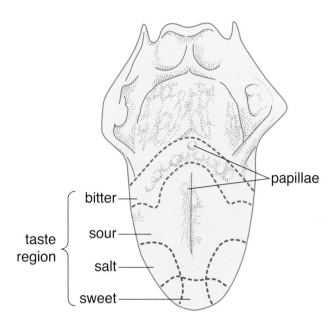

Figure 2

In the United States, about 70 percent of the population can taste PTC. There is no significant difference in tasting ability between males and females. People who dislike broccoli, cauliflower, and cabbage are generally tasters. In addition, the majority of smokers are nontasters.

The allele that enables one to taste the sulfur-containing chemical PTC was once believed to show simple mendelian dominance to the allele for nontasting. Geneticists now know that the taster allele shows *incomplete dominance*. People who inherit a taster allele from both parents are more sensitive to PTC than those who inherit one taster allele and one nontaster allele.

Connections

The ability to taste different bitter compounds is influenced by almost 30 genes. However, the presence of the taster gene for PTC correlates to one's sensitivity to other bitter compounds. Since people generally do not like bitter foods, one might wonder why the gene to taste bitterness has been passed on for thousands of years. The answer may be found in early humans' diet. Some poisonous plants contain bitter chemicals that discourage herbivores. Therefore, natural selection preserved the genes for tasting bitter compounds because they helped ensure survival.

Most grazing animals are not as sensitive to the range of tastes that people can experience, especially bitter tastes. The digestive systems of animals that eat bitter, toxic plants deal with the dangerous chemicals after they are ingested. Many grazers have large livers, much larger to those of humans, to process and remove toxic compounds.

Want to Know More?

See appendix for Our Findings.

Further Reading

Chudler, Eric. "That's Tasty," December 4, 2009. Neuroscience for Kids. Available online. URL: http://faculty.washington.edu/chudler/tasty.html. Accessed February 10, 2010. This Web site does a great job of explaining how we sense taste.

"Supertaster's Taste Game." *Scientific American Frontiers*. Available online. URL: http://www.pbs.org/saf/1105/features/taste.htm. Accessed December 14, 2009. This interactive Web site enables you to compare the reactions of "normal" and "super" tasters to certain foods.

Wooding, Stephen. "Natural Selection at Work in Genetic Variation to Taste," *Medical News Today*, June 28, 2004. Available online. URL: http://www.medicalnewstoday.com/articles/10009.php. Accessed December 13, 2009. In this article, Wooding explains how and why the ability to taste bitter compounds served as a selective advantage for early humans.

8. Using Karyotypes to Diagnose Conditions

Topic

Homologous chromosomes have similar banding patterns and can be identified visually.

Introduction

A *karyotype* is a test that shows a picture of a person's chromosomes. Figure 1 shows the karyotype of a normal female. Notice that there are 23 pairs of chromosomes, arranged in order. The last two chromosomes, pair 23, are both Xs. If this were the karyotype of a male, the last two chromosomes would be an X and a Y. The Y chromosome is much smaller than the X. A karyotype reveals whether or not there are any chromosomes with extra, missing, or broken parts. A person may want a karyotype to see if he or she has a chromosomal abnormality that can be passed on to offspring. Women who have had miscarriages may request a karyotype to see if there is a chromosomal reason for the problem. Sometimes expectant parents need a karyotype of a fetus to see if it has a chromosomal defect. If a baby is born with ambiguous genitalia, a karyotype can help determine whether the child is male or female. Some of the most common genetic disorders determined by karyotyping include following:

- ✔ Klinefelter's syndrome, in which a male (XY) has an extra X chromosome.
- ✔ Turner's syndrome, a condition in which a female has only one X chromosome.
- ✔ *Down syndrome*, which is caused by an extra chromosome 21.
- ✔ Patau's syndrome, which is due to an extra chromosome 13.
- ✔ Edward's syndrome, a condition that results from three copies of chromosome 18.

To prepare a karyotype, body cells are collected and raised in culture until they begin undergoing cell division. During cell division, chromosomes, which are normally long and thin, condense into thick structures that can be seen clearly and photographed under the microscope. The individual chromosomes in the photo are cut out and arranged in matching pairs from 1 to 23. Chromosomes can be identified by their light and dark bands. Stains used in karyotyping make the adenine-thymine regions of the chromosomes dark. In this experiment, you will cut out and arrange paper "chromosomes" with abnormalities and compare them to a normal set.

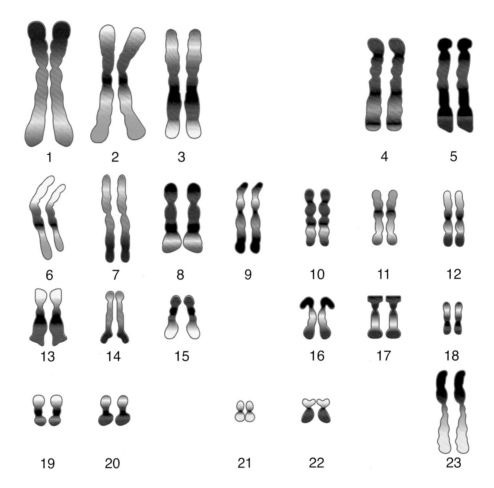

Figure 1

Karyotype of a normal female

Time Required

45 minutes

Materials

➡️ scissors

➡️ tape or glue

➥   Photocopies of Figures 2 and 3 (in color, if possible)

➥   science notebook

Safety Note Take care when working with scissors. Please review and follow the safety guidelines at the beginning of this volume.

Procedure

1. Answer Analysis questions 1 and 2.

2. Examine Figure 1 on page 48, which shows chromosomes from a normal female. Answer Analysis questions 3 through 6.

3. Figure 2 shows the chromosomes of a fetus with a chromosomal abnormality. Cut out the chromosomes from a photocopy of the figure and arrange them in pairs. Compare the chromosomes to those in Figure 1. Answer Analysis questions 7 through 9.

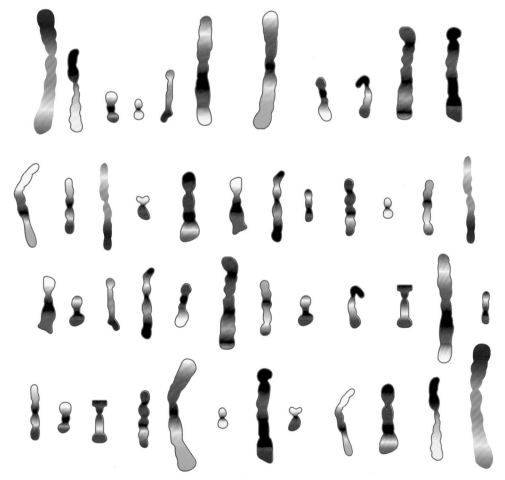

Figure 2

Chromosomes of a fetus

4. Figure 3 shows the chromosomes of a young male. Cut out the chromosomes from a photocopy of the figure and arrange them in pairs. Compare the chromosomes to those in Figure 1. Answer Analysis question 10.

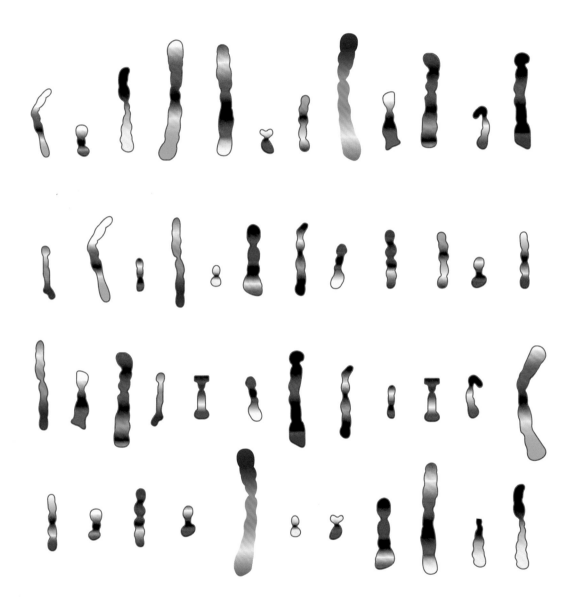

Figure 3

Chromosomes of a young male

Analysis

1. Why might a couple want a karyotype of their fetus?
2. How do male and female karyotypes differ?

3. How many chromosomes does the individual in Figure 1 have? How many were inherited from that person's mother? How many from the father?

4. A complete set of chromosomes is referred to as the *diploid number*. What is the diploid number in Figure 1?

5. A half set of chromosomes is the *haploid number*. What is the haploid number in Figure 1?

6. All of the chromosomes except X and Y are called *autosomes*. How many autosomes does an individual have?

7. Is the individual shown in Figure 2 male or female? How do you know?

8. How do the chromosomes in Figure 2 differ from those in Figure 1?

9. Name the syndrome shown in Figure 2.

10. How do the chromosomes in Figure 3 differ from those in Figure 1?

What's Going On?

In this experiment, you carried out the job of a geneticist by cutting out pictures of chromosomes, arranging them in pairs, then examining them to see if any abnormalities exist. The first karyotype you examined (Figure 2) was from a female fetus who has an extra chromosome 21. This child will have the condition Down syndrome, or trisomy 21. About one in every 800 babies shows this defect. Children with Down syndrome show developmental delays both physically and mentally.

Figure 3 shows the chromosomes of a male with Klinefelter's syndrome caused by an extra X chromosome. Klinefelter's is one of the most common chromosomal abnormalities, occurring in one out of 500 births. In many cases, the presence of the extra X does not cause any symptoms. In other cases, production of testosterone is lower than normal, so these males are infertile and generally have less facial and body hair than normal males.

Connections

Women over 35 are more likely to have children with trisomy conditions than younger women. This is because as women age, their eggs are more likely to make a mistake in *meiosis*, or reduction division that produces egg and sperm. The precursor cells to egg and sperm have 46 chromosomes. When these cells undergo meiosis, their chromosome number is reduced by half. Each reproductive cell ends up with just 23 chromosomes. If an error occurs and some of the chromosomes get stuck together, meiosis may produce one cell with an extra chromosome and another that is missing a chromosome.

Several testing options are available to mature women. *Ultrasound*, the use of high-pitched sounds waves to create a visual image of the embryo, can find some birth defects. However, this test cannot analyze the chromosomes. *Chorionic villus sampling (CVS)* and *amniocentesis* are tests that collect some of the embryonic cells before birth for karyotyping. CVS can be carried out early, around weeks 11 and 12. Amniocentesis can be performed between weeks 15 and 20. Women who may be interested in the tests must weigh the benefits of knowing their babies' karyotypes against the risks of the tests themselves.

Want to Know More?

See appendix for Our Findings.

Further Reading

"Karyotyping," 2009. HowStuffWorks. Available online. URL: http://healthguide.howstuffworks.com/karyotyping-dictionary.htm. Accessed December 19, 2009. This Web site explains how tissue for a karyotype is collected, how to prepare for the test, and what kind of results you can expect from the test.

Leshin, Len. "Down Syndrome: Health Issues," January 2007. Available online. URL: http://www.ds-health.com/. Accessed December 19, 2009. Leshin, the parent of a Down syndrome child, created this Web site to help students understand the condition. Prenatal testing, health concerns, and an explanation of why the disorder occurs are some of the topics discussed by Dr. Leshin.

"Spectral Karyotyping," December 17, 2009. National Human Genome Research Institute. Available online. URL: http://www.genome.gov/10000208. Accessed December 19, 2009. This Web site by the National Institutes of Health explains a technique in which pairs of chromosomes are "painted" unique colors for easy analysis.

9. Extracting DNA From Cheek Cells

Topic

All cells in the body, except for red blood cells, contain DNA.

Introduction

Deoxyribonucleic acid (DNA) is a large organic molecule that carries the genetic information in a cell. Found in fungi, bacteria, protozoans, plants, and animals, this molecule determines the traits of an organism. Your DNA codes for all the characteristics that make you human, as well as the traits that make you a unique individual. Less than 0.1 percent of your DNA is different from the DNA of another person.

In the cells of all eukaryotic organisms, DNA is contained within a nucleus. Each DNA molecule is a long, thin thread. When a cell prepares to divide, the DNA condenses into short, thick chromosomes to facilitate reshuffling. Humans have 46 chromosomes, or 23 pairs. The DNA molecule is a double helix made of chains of subunits called *nucleotides* (see Figure 1). Each nucleotide has three basic parts: a nitrogenous base, a sugar, and a phosphate group. In all cases, the sugar and phosphate group are the same, but there are four different bases: adenine (A), guanine (G), thymine (T), and cytosine (C). The genetic code is determined by the arrangement of these bases.

In this experiment, you will collect some cells from the inside of your mouth, then isolate the DNA from these cells.

Time Required

45 minutes

Materials

- ⟶ 1 test tube
- ⟶ 2 grams (g) salt (sodium chloride)

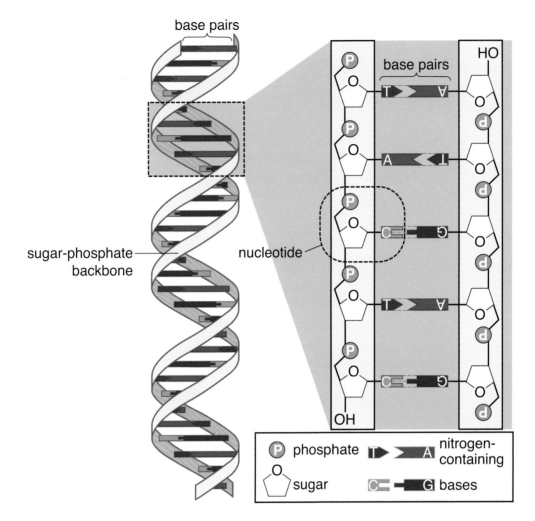

Figure 1

- ➻ 1 milliliter (ml) liquid soap (the type used to wash dishes)

- ➻ 1/2 test tube of chilled ethanol (95 percent)

- ➻ distilled water (about 50 ml)

- ➻ 2 small paper cups

- ➻ graduated cylinder

- ➻ stirring rod

- ➻ small piece of plastic wrap

- ➻ science notebook

Safety Note Take care when working with ethanol, which is extremely flammable. Please review and follow the safety guidelines at the beginning of this volume.

Procedure

1. Pour 10 ml of distilled water into one of the small paper cups. Add about 1 g of salt and stir.
2. Pour 3 ml of distilled water into the other small paper cup. Add 1 ml of liquid soap and stir.
3. Swish the salt water around your mouth for 1 minute.
4. Spit the water back into the paper cup.
5. Pour the swished salt water into the test tube.
6. Add about 1 ml of the soap solution to the test tube.
7. Cover the top of the test tube with a small piece of plastic wrap and shake gently until well mixed.
8. Remove the plastic wrap and pour the chilled 95 percent ethanol into the test tube. Do not stir or mix.
9. Observe the test tube for several minutes. The DNA will float to the interface of the salt-soap solution and the alcohol. You can remove the DNA by swirling it around a stirring rod.

Analysis

1. What is DNA?
2. From whom did you inherit your DNA?
3. A DNA molecule is a chain made up of thousands of subunits called nucleotides. Describe a nucleotide.
4. Describe the appearance of the DNA you collected in this experiment.
5. Where did the DNA in this experiment come from?
6. Suggest some other sources of your DNA.

What's Going On?

Even though DNA is a relatively large molecule, it cannot be seen with the naked eye. In this experiment, you produced a clump made of trillions of DNA strands. When you swished water in your mouth, you picked up some of the *epithelial cells* lining your checks. You exposed the cells to two chemicals, salt and detergent. The dish washing detergent broke open the cell membranes, releasing the DNA into the solution. Both the detergent and the salt removed proteins that are associated with DNA. When you poured alcohol on top of the salt-detergent-cell mixture, everything except the DNA dissolved. DNA is not very soluble in cold alcohol, so it precipitated out of solution, collecting at the point where the alcohol and the solution meet.

Connections

One of the easiest ways to gather DNA from an individual is through a *buccal* or cheek swab. In this test, a sterile cotton swab (see Figure 2) is rubbed across the inside of the cheek to collect cells. The DNA in these cells can then be analyzed. DNA can be collected with buccal swabs for several purposes. Police may use a buccal swab to compare the DNA of a suspect to the DNA collected at a crime scene. Buccal swabs can also be used to establish paternity if the father of a child is not known. In addition, buccal swabs can help establish gender if a child is born with a combination of male and female genitals, which can make gender hard to identify.

Want to Know More?

See appendix for Our Findings.

Figure 2

To collect DNA, a sterile swap is rubbed across the inside of the cheeks: The swab is then placed in a plastic container and sent to the lab.

Further Reading

"Baking Out DNA: Forensic Scientists Improve DNA Analysis With Mummy-inspired Bone-baking," February 1, 2008. *ScienceDaily*. Available online. URL: http://www.sciencedaily.com/videos/2008/0201-baking_out_dna. htm. Accessed December 19, 2009. *ScienceDaily* provides an article, video, and narration on techniques for removing DNA from bones of mummies.

Clark, Jim. "DNA Structure," 2007. Chemguide. Available online. URL: http://www.chemguide.co.uk/organicprops/aminoacids/dna1.html. Accessed December 19, 2009. Clark provides information on inorganic chemistry as well as organic molecules such as DNA.

"3D DNA Explorer," 2003. PBS. Available online. URL: http://www.pbs. org/wnet/dna/dna_explorer/index2.html. Accessed December 19, 2009. This interactive Web site lets you manipulate a model of a DNA double helix, turning it and clicking on atoms of interest.

10. Design an Organism's Traits

Topic

Some traits are inherited as dominant and recessive alleles, while others show incomplete dominance, codominance, or sex-linkage.

Introduction

When Austrian monk Gregor Mendel (1822–84) carried out his experiments with pea plants, he found that the some traits mask others. For example, he learned that if the trait for tallness is present, it hides the trait for shortness. He referred to the traits that mask others as *dominant* and the ones that are masked as *recessive*. Today we know that the traits Mendel studied are controlled by two forms or *alleles* of genes. The genes that an organism possesses make up its *genotype*. The appearance of an organism because of its genes is its *phenotype*.

Since Mendel's time, other types of inheritance have been discovered. For example, some traits are described as *codominant* because both traits are completely expressed. In horses and cattle, coat color can show codominance. If an animal inherits one dominant allele for red hair in the coat (R) and another dominant allele for white hair (W), both colors of hair are expressed. The animal has red and white hairs in the coat, producing a coloration known as *roan*.

In another form of inheritance, *incomplete dominance*, two traits are inherited but neither are fully dominant. As a result, the traits produce a blended effect. A cross between a red-flowering snapdragon (R) and a white-flowering plant (W) yields offspring that are pink-flowering (RW) (see Figure 1).

Some genes are located on the X chromosome. These genes are described as sex-linked because females (XX) inherit two copies and males (XY) inherit one. Red-green color blindness is one example of a sex-linked trait. The gene for color vision is found on the X chromosome. The recessive allele (c) causes colorblindness and the dominant allele (C) yields normal color vision. A female with one recessive gene (X^cX^c) has normal color vision but a male with one recessive gene (X^cY) is color blind.

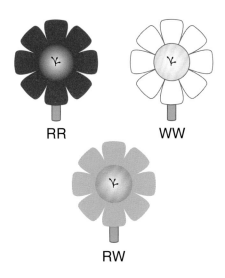

Figure 1

If a pure-breeding red snapdragon (RR) is crossed with a pure-breeding white plant (WW), the offspring produce pink (RW) flowers.

In this experiment, you will design a fictitious organism—a monster— to find out how different modes of inheritance affect phenotype.

Time Required

45 minutes

Materials

- 2 yellow index cards (or squares of card stock)
- 2 blue index cards (or squares of card stock)
- 2 green index cards (or squares of card stock)
- 2 red index cards (or squares of card stock)
- 2 purple index cards (or squares of card stock)
- scissors
- colored pencils
- science notebook

Procedure

1. Your job is to design a monster with five distinct genetic traits. List the traits you want to give your monster in your science notebook.

2. Assign each of the five traits a type of inheritance. To do so:

    a. Decide which two traits will have simple dominant and recessive alleles. For example, you may decide to let horns be one of the traits inherited by simple dominance. If so, write "horns" on the data table, on page 62 under "Simple dominance" in the row titled "Traits." Decide what genes you will assign to horns. For example, you could let H represent a dominant gene for horns and h stand for a recessive gene for no horns. Write the genes you want to use in the same column in the row titled "Genes."

    b. Select another trait that will be inherited by simple dominance and add it to the data table in column "Simple dominance." Write the traits in the row titled "Trait" and the genes you want to use in the row titled "Genes."

    c. Decide which of your monster's traits will show codominance and write it on the data table in the "Trait" row in column "Codominance." Write the genes you want to use in the row titled "Genes." In codominance, both genes are written as capital letters.

    d. Select a trait to be controlled by incomplete dominance. Write the trait and the genes for this is on the data table in column "Incomplete dominance." In incomplete dominance, both genes are written as capital letters.

    e. The last trait must be sex-linked. Write this trait and the genes on the data table in column "Sex-linked." The genes can be dominant or recessive. Write the genes as superscripts on the X chromosome. The Y chromosome does not carry a sex-linked trait.

3. On the data table, complete the row titled "Possible genotypes," the possible combinations of the genes, for each type of inheritance. For the example used in procedure step 1, the possible genotypes are HH, Hh, and hh.

4. On the data table, complete the row titled "Possible phenotypes," the possible traits from the genotypes in the row above. The phenotypes for the example in procedure step 1 would be "horns" or "no horns."

5. The index cards represent the chromosomes of your organism. Two cards of the same color are *homologous chromosomes*, similar in size and structure but from different parents. Assign genes to the cards. To do so:

   a. On one of the yellow cards, write the two genes for one of the traits from column "Simple dominance." Write one gene on each side. Write the same thing on the second yellow card. For example, if the trait of horns shows simple dominance, you would write "H" on one side of each card and "h" on the other side of each card.

   b. On one of the blue cards, write the two genes for "Simple dominance," one gene on each side of the card. Write the same thing on the second blue card.

   c. On one of the green cards, write the two genes for "Codominance." Write one gene on each side of the card. For example, if the trait for hair color is codominant, write P for purple on one side and G for green on the other side. Write the same thing on the second green card.

   d. On one of the red cards, write the two genes for "Incomplete dominance." Write one gene on each side of the card. For example, if the gene for long fingers is L and the gene for short fingers is S, write L on one side of the card and S on the other. Write the same thing on the second red card.

   e. The purple cards show sex-linked inheritance. Write X on one side of a purple card and Y on the other side. On the second card, write X on both sides. Then go back and add the traits that you created for "Sex-linked" on the X chromosomes. You can write the trait as dominant (capital letter) or as recessive (lower case letter).

6. To find out your monster's traits, throw all of the cards up in the air. This represents the mixing of alleles from your monster's parents.

7. Without flipping over any cards, pair up the colors.

8. Examine the two yellow cards. If either of the cards shows the dominant gene, your monster will have that trait. If both cards show the recessive gene, you monster will show that trait. Record your monster's trait on the data table.

Data Table

	Simple dominance	Simple dominance	Co-dominance	Incomplete dominance	Sex-linked
Traits					
Genes					
Possible genotypes					
Possible phenotypes					
Card color	Yellow	Blue	Green	Red	Purple
Your monster's traits					

9. Examine the two blue cards. If either of the cards shows the dominant gene, your monster will have the trait. If both cards show the recessive gene, you monster will show that trait. Record your monster's trait on the data table.

10. Examine the two green cards. If the genes are the same, your monster will show the trait. However, if the genes are different, both traits will be expressed. Record your monster's trait on the data table.

11. Examine the two red cards. If the genes are the same on both cards, your monster will show that trait. However, if the genes are different, your monster will show a blend of both traits. Record your monster's trait on the data table.

12. Examine the purple cards. Determine whether your monster is male or female. Then decide if the dominant or recessive gene is expressed. Record your monster's trait on the data table.

13. Now that you know the traits of your monster, draw it in your science notebook.

14. In your science notebook, write a description of your monster. Describe how its genetic traits are important the monster's day-to-day activities.

Analysis

1. What type of inheritance did Mendel see in his pea plants: simple dominance, codominance, incomplete dominance, or sex-linked?

2. Explain the difference between codominant traits and traits that are incompletely dominant.

3. Why do sex-linked recessive traits appear more often in males than females?

4. What represented the monster's chromosomes in this experiment?

5. What represented the monster's genes in this experiment?

6. How does this experiment about monster genetics relate to real life?

What's Going On?

In this experiment, you worked with several types of inheritance to show how a fictitious organism inherited its genetic traits. Since you designed the monster, you could have assigned it any traits. For example, you may have decided that warts on the face (W) are dominant over no warts (w). This trait could result in only two genotypes: warts on the face (WW and Ww) and no warts on the face (ww) (see Figure 2). Pointed ears in monsters (P) might be dominant over round ears (p). Hair straightness in monsters might be codominant. Straight hair is S, curly hair is C. A monster that inherits one S and one C would have some straight hair and some curly hair. Color in monsters might show incomplete dominance. Red (R) and White (W) monsters might produce pink offspring (RW). A sex-linked trait might be associated with monster appendages, arms or wings, with arms (A) dominant over wings (a). Most females would show the dominant trait A for arms because females with the genotypes $X^A X^A$ and $X^A X^a$ would have arms. To have wings, a female must inherit two recessive genes, $X^a X^a$. Males with genotype $X^A Y$ would have arms and $X^a Y$ would have wings.

Connections

In humans, several types of inheritance are seen. Traits governed by simple dominance include freckles, the shape of the hairline, and the ability to roll the tongue. Incomplete dominance determines whether hair will be straight, curly, or wavy. If an offspring inherits the gene for straight hair from one parent and the gene for curly hair from another parent, the result will be wavy hair. The inheritance of blood type is controlled by codominant genes. There are three alleles for blood type, A, B, and O. The types A and B are both dominant; O is recessive. If an offspring inherits two A alleles, or an A and an O allele, they will have type A blood. Similarly, if an offspring inherits two B alleles, or a B and an O allele, their blood type will be type B. However, if an A and a B allele are inherited, both are expressed and the blood type is AB. Sex-linked traits in humans include color vision and *hemophilia*, a blood disease.

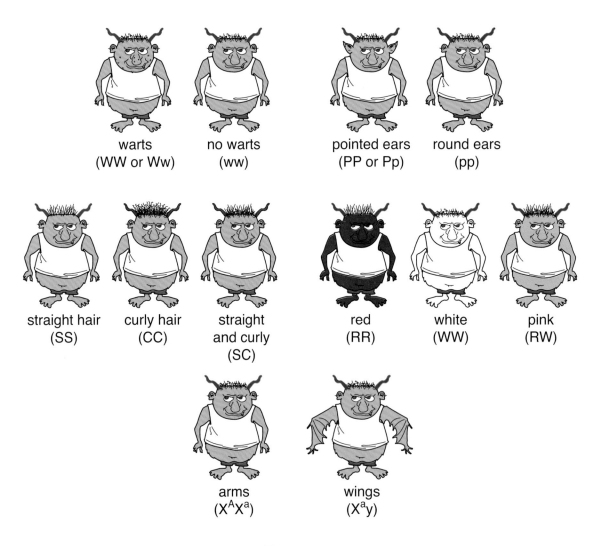

warts
(WW or Ww)

no warts
(ww)

pointed ears
(PP or Pp)

round ears
(pp)

straight hair
(SS)

curly hair
(CC)

straight
and curly
(SC)

red
(RR)

white
(WW)

pink
(RW)

arms
($X^A X^a$)

wings
($X^a y$)

Figure 2

Want to Know More?

See appendix for Our Findings.

Further Reading

"Basic Genetics." Think Quest. Available online. URL: http://library. thinkquest.org/20465/genes.html. Accessed December 20, 2009. This student-developed Web site does a good job of explaining how traits are inherited.

Bowling, Sue Ann. *Animal Genetics*, 2000. Available online. URL: http:// bowlingsite.mcf.com/genetics/Genetics.html. Accessed December 20, 2009. Bowling is a scientist and author who provides simple explanations of different types of inheritance in dogs in her online textbook.

O'Neil, Dennis. *Biological Basis for Heredity: An Introduction to Basic Cell Structures Related to Genetic Inheritance*. Available online. URL: http:// anthro.palomar.edu/biobasis/default.htm. O'Neil provides extensive information on inheritance, including the way sex-linked traits are passed from parents to offspring in this Web textbook.

11. Chromosomal Mutations

Topic

Models can be used to demonstrate types of chromosomal mutations.

Introduction

Your genetic information is carried on 23 pairs of chromosomes located in the nucleus of almost every cell in your body. Each chromosome is a long molecule of deoxyribonucleic acid (DNA). Genes are segments of chromosomes that tell your body how to function; your chromosomes contain about 25,000 genes.

All your chromosomes have some similar characteristics. Each one has a short section, the p arm, and a long section, the q arm, that are separated by a pinched-in region, the *centromere*. When chromosomes are stained, each shows distinctive patterns of dark and light bands (see Figure 1). The bands are numbered and can be used as reference points for identification.

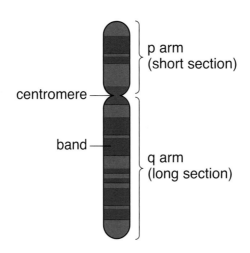

centromere

band

p arm
(short section)

q arm
(long section)

Figure 1

Any change in DNA is referred to as a *mutation*. Sometimes DNA is damaged or changed when it is passed on to offspring. At other times, a chromosomal alteration occurs in a fetus. Types of chromosomal mutations include *deletions*, *duplications*, *inversions*, *translocations*, and *reciprocal translocations*. If a deletion occurs, part of a chromosome is removed, along with the genetic information on that chromosome. The larger the deletion, the more DNA lost and the more severe the consequences. A deletion can happen on either arm of any chromosome, and it can be of any size.

In a duplication, a section of DNA on a chromosome is copied so that too much DNA is present. Some duplications produce *trisomies* because the genes involved in the duplication are present in sets of three. In an inversion, a section of DNA is deleted then reinserted in a reversed position. This type of change affects the way some genes are expressed. A translocation occurs when a section of DNA is lost from one chromosome and inserted into another one. This type of mutation affects gene expression. If the translocation is reciprocal, sections of DNA are removed from two different chromosomes and their positions switched. In this experiment, you will create models of chromosomal mutations.

Time Required

45 minutes

Materials

- scissors
- glue or tape
- photocopy of Figure 2 (in color, if possbile)
- sheet of paper
- science notebook

Safety Note Take care when working with scissors. Please review and follow the safety guidelines at the beginning of this volume.

Procedure

1. Copy the data table in your science notebook.

2. Figure 2 provides several copies of chromosomes that you will use in this lesson. Cut out chromosome A from the photocopy of Figure 2. Alter chromosome A to show how it might look if a deletion occurred. To do so, remove the highlighted section, then tape the chromosome back together. Tape or glue the altered chromosome to any row on the right side of the data table in your science notebook. (When you finish gluing chromosomes on your data table, you will give it to another student and ask the student to identify the type of mutation that has occurred. For this reason, do not put the first chromosome in the first row, the second chromosome in the second row, and so forth.)

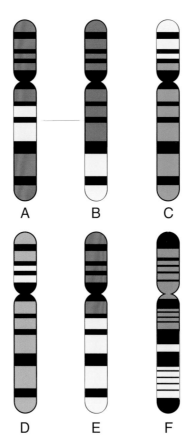

A   B   C

D   E   F

Figure 2

3. Cut out chromosome B. Draw another copy of the highlighted portion of this chromosome on a sheet of paper. Cut open the chromosome just above the highlighted area and insert the duplicated section that you drew. Tape the chromosome back together with the duplicated region. Tape or glue the altered chromosome to any row on the right side of the data table.

4. Cut out chromosome C. Then cut out the highlighted area, turn it upside down, and replace it in the chromosome. Tape the chromosome back together. Tape or glue the altered chromosome to any row on the right side of the data table.

5. Cut out chromosome D, remove the highlighted section, and throw it away. On a sheet of paper, draw a different chromosome section and tape it to the place where the highlighted section used to be. Tape or glue the altered chromosome to any row on the right side of the data table.

6. Cut out chromosomes E and F, remove the highlighted sections, and switch their positions on the two chromosomes. Tape or glue the altered chromosomes in any row on the right side of the data table.

7. Swap data tables with another student. In the left-hand column of the other student's data table, write the names of the types of mutations that are glued in the right-hand column.

8. Check with the person who created the data table to see if you named the chromosomal mutations correctly.

Analysis

1. Which of the chromosomal abnormalities results in loss of genetic information?

2. Some genes are turned on or activated by adjacent genes. How might an inversion affect these genes?

3. *Point mutations* involve only one region within one gene. How is a point mutation different from a chromosomal mutation?

4. Which do you think will cause the most severe changes, a deletion or a translocation? Explain your reasoning.

What's Going On?

In this experiment, you examined some of the changes that can occur in chromosomes. Although in some cases changes are passed from parent to child, most often they occur spontaneously in the fetus. A new mutation in a fetus is called a *de novo* abnormality. In either case, alterations to chromosomes can have various effects on the individual, depending on which chromosomes and how many genes are involved. Loss of DNA in a deletion causes more severe changes than rearrangement of chromosomes. One example of a chromosomal disorder caused by a

Data Table	
Name of chromosomal mutation	**Altered chromosomes**

partial or complete deletion of the short arm of chromosome 5 is *cri du chat syndrome*. The loss of such a large portion of DNA causes multiple symptoms, including a high-pitched, cat-like cry for which the syndrome is named. Children born with this abnormality may experience delayed development, intellectual disability, *microcephaly*, weak muscle tone, and distinctive facial features. Intellectual disability is most likely due to the loss of a particular gene, CTNND2, which functions in development of organized nerve cells. After birth, the gene plays a critically important role in transmission of nerve impulses.

Connections

From one generation to the next, the amount of genetic change that occurs in a population is small. However, over time, the number of changes accumulates, creating significant alternations in the population's genes. Eventually, changes can lead to the evolution of a new species. In plants, if two slightly different species cross pollinate, the offspring may retain some extra copies of several or all of the chromosomes. An extra set of chromosomes, a condition known as *polyploidy*, is fairly common in plants. Some scientists estimate that up to 70 percent of all flowering plants are polyploids. For example, there are several species of coffee plants with polyploid chromosomes. The ancestral variety has 22 chromosomes, but other species have 44, 66, and 88. Scientists believe the other species are polyploids that developed from the ancestral form. This same type of chromosomal mutations also occurs in some animals, including insects, fish, and amphibians. One of the few species of polyploid mammals is a rat from Argentina. The cells of the polyploid organism are much larger than those of the normal rat because they contain more DNA than normal cells.

Want to Know More?

See appendix for Our Findings.

Further Reading

Armstrong, W. P. "Polyploidy and Hybridization in San Diego County," 2008. Available online. URL: http://waynesword.palomar.edu/hybrids1. htm. Accessed January 4, 2010. On this Web page, Armstrong explains how new species develop with polyploid chromosomes and discusses the procedure for making a fertile polyploid hybrid.

"Chromosome 18 Registry and Research Society," 2009. Available online. URL: http://chromosome18.org/Conditions/Genetics/ FAQsAboutChromosomeAbnormalities/tabid/117/Default.aspx. Accessed December 22, 2009. This Web site explains problems caused by abnormalities of chromosome 18.

"Prenatal Diagnosis." The Internet Pathology Laboratory for Medical Education. Available online. URL: http://library.med.utah.edu/WebPath/ TUTORIAL/PRENATAL/PRENATAL.html. Accessed December 22, 2009. Mercer University School of Medicine, Savannah, Georgia, provides a web resource with tutorials on many topics including chromosomal abnormalities.

12. The Traits of Parents and Offspring Are Not Identical

Topic

Fruit flies can be crossed to demonstrate trends in dominant and recessive traits over a period of three generations.

Introduction

Your physical traits, such as your hair color, eye color, and height, came from your forebears. These traits are located on *genes*, segments of chromosomal DNA that carry the instructions for making the proteins that determine every detail of how you are constructed. You received one set of chromosomes from your mother and another complimentary set from your father. Some of your traits result from a dominant form or *allele* of these genes, which means that they are always expressed. Other traits are controlled by recessive alleles, so they will only be expressed when there is not a dominant trait present.

The particular combination of genes in an individual is known as his or her *genotype*. If two dominant genes are present, the genotype is *homozygous* dominant. If there are two recessive traits, it is homozygous recessive. One dominant and one recessive gene creates a *heterozygous* genotype. Heterozygous individuals always express the dominant trait, even though they are carrying a gene for a recessive trait.

To understand how dominant and recessive genes work, consider the trait for dimples. There are two alleles of this gene: the dominant allele (D) for dimples and the recessive allele (d) for no dimples. Individuals with DD or Dd genotypes express the dimpled trait, but those with the dd genotype do not have dimples.

A Punnett square can determine the probability of offspring having certain genotypes and expressing certain phenotypes, or appearance. The punnett square in Figure 1 shows the cross between two individuals that are heterozygous for a trait. Their offspring have a 75 percent chance of expressing the dominant trait and a 25 percent chance of expressing the recessive trait, a phenotypic ratio of 3:1. In this experiment, you will breed fruit flies, *Drosophila melanogaster*, and observe the phenotypes that are present in two generations of offspring from parental generations

Procedure, Part B

1. Create a mating vial labeled "F1 generation" that contains medium on which the flies will lay eggs. Combine one part drosophila medium with one part water. Stir to mix and place in the bottom of a vial with a stopper. Allow the medium to dry before adding flies.

2. Anesthetize and separate the recently hatched males and females from the stock vials. (Ideally, this should be done within 8 hours of hatching.)

3. Place four males and four females into a new mating vial labeled F1 generation. Either use four wild-type females (w.t.f.) and four mutant males (m.m.) or four mutant females (m.f.) and four wild-type males (w.t.m.). Label your mating vial appropriately. Allow the adults to mate and lay eggs for several days to a week.

Procedure, Part C

1. After 8 to 10 days, anesthetize the adults, remove them from the vial, and place them in the morgue.

2. Create a new breeding vial filled with fresh drosophila medium labeled F2 generation.

3. After another 8 to 10 days, the flies from the F1 generation (first generation of offspring) will begin to emerge. As the flies hatch, anesthetize them and observe their phenotypes (wild type or mutant). Record this information on the data table on the row labeled "F1 generation."

4. From the emerging flies, place about four males and four virgin females into a new F2 (second offspring) generation vial. (Place remaining flies in the morgue.)

5. After the majority of F2 generation of flies has hatched, generally about 10 days, anesthetize and sort onto index cards according to their phenotypes. Complete the data table.

6. At the conclusion of the laboratory, dispose of all flies in the morgue unless otherwise instructed by the teacher.

Analysis

1. Draw two Punnett squares predicting the expected results for each of the crosses completed in this lab (the first between the two pure-breeding strands, and the second between the offspring of the first cross).

Data Table		
	Number of wild-type flies	**Number of mutant flies**
F1 generation		
F2 generation		

2. Using the results recorded on the data table, calculate the percentage of flies showing each phenotype. To find percentage, divide the number of flies of that phenotype by the total number of flies, then multiply the results by 100. The formula for this calculation is:

$$\text{percentage} = \frac{\text{number flies of that phenotype}}{\text{total number of flies}} \times 100$$

3. Were the actual percentages similar to what was expected based on the punnett squares? Why or why not?

4. Combine your data from the F2 generation with all of the data from the class and recalculate the percentages for each phenotype.

5. Were the results any different using a larger sample of flies? Explain.

6. If you had collected data after only a few flies had hatched from the F2 generation, how might your data have been different?

7. When doing a statistical analysis to determine how closely a population follows what is expected, why is it beneficial to have a large sample of organisms?

What's Going On?

Gregor Mendel (1822–84) is known as the father of modern genetics because of his research in the late 1800s involving pea plants. Mendel was an Austrian monk who noticed a pattern in the traits that were passed on in pea plants. Mendel calculated the numbers of pea plants with certain characteristics and noted that the ratio of dominant "factors" to recessive ones was about 3:1. These results are due to what Mendel called the *law of segregation*, which states that each parent has two factors that separate from each other when sex cells are formed. Those factors can unite with factors from the other parent to form many different combinations. Today, scientists know that the factors are genes on chromosomes that are separated from each other during *meiosis*.

Although the phenotypic ratio of dominant to recessive traits resulting from a heterozygous cross is generally around 3:1, the genotypic ratio is 1:2:1. Approximately 25 percent of the offspring are expected to have a homozygous dominant genotype, 50 percent are expected to have a heterozygous genotype, and 25 percent are expected to have a homozygous recessive genotype. However, it is not possible to distinguish visually a homozygous dominant and heterozygous individual because both genotypes express the same traits. The organisms must undergo a special type mating known as a *testcross* to determine their genotypes.

Connections

Recessive genes cause many human disorders such as albinism, cystic fibrosis, and sickle cell anemia. When recessive genetic disorders appear, parents are often surprised because neither of them may show the traits. For this reason, some individuals participate in genetic testing and counseling before they decide to have children. People who have a family history of genetic disorders often have their DNA tested to determine if they are carriers of the recessive allele that may affect their potential offspring. Genetic counselors can review the results of genetic testing of both parents and discuss the probability of having a child that is affected with certain disorders. After obtaining information from genetic counselors, couples can make informed choices as to whether they want to have children naturally, or adopt.

 ## Want to Know More?

See appendix for Our Findings.

Further Reading

Fancher, Lynn J. "Solving Genetics Problems I: Monohybrid Cross," 2000. Available online. URL: http://www.cod.edu/PEOPLE/FACULTY/FANCHER/ GenProb1.htm. Accessed January 9, 2010. Fancher explains how to use Punnett squares and pedigrees in analyzing monohybrid crosses on this Web page.

"Mendelian Laws of Inheritance," 2010. Science Clarified. Available online. URL: http://www.scienceclarified.com/Ma-Mu/Mendelian-Laws-of-Inheritance.html. Accessed January 7, 2010. This Web site discusses Mendel's laws and explains how to predict the traits of offspring.

"Mutant Flies." Exploratorium. Available online. URL: http://www.exploratorium.edu/exhibits/mutant_flies/mutant_flies.html. Accessed January 7, 2010. This Web site provides figures and descriptions of several types of mutant fruit flies that can be used in genetics experiments.

"Tour of the Basics," 2010. Learn.Genetics. Available online. URL: http://learn.genetics.utah.edu/content/begin/tour/. Accessed on June 17, 2010. Provided by the University of Utah, this Web site explains genes, traits, and inheritance.

13. Transmission of Sex-linked Mutations

Topic

Fruit flies can be crossed to demonstrate transmission of sex-linked traits.

Introduction

Genes, sections of DNA that determine an organism's traits, are found on chromosomes. Humans have 23 pairs of chromosomes. Twenty-two pairs, the *autosomal chromosomes*, determine traits that are not related to the gender of an individual. One pair, the sex chromosomes, determines whether an individual is male or female. A female has two X chromosomes while a male has one X and one Y. The X chromosome is relatively large and also carries several traits unrelated to gender. Because it is much smaller, the Y chromosome carries very few additional traits. Genes located on the X chromosome are described as *sex-linked*.

Fruit flies, *Drosophila melanogaster*, are often used in genetic studies because they reproduce quickly and are easy to maintain and study. Fruit flies have four pairs of chromosomes: three pairs of autosomes and one pair of sex chromosomes. The sex chromosomes in fruit flies are very similar to those in humans in both the determination of sex and the number of traits carried on the X and Y chromosomes.

Sex-linked traits can be predicted using punnett squares. Sex-linked traits are written as superscripts on the X (see Figure 1). In this experiment, you will predict the outcome of crosses in fruit flies, and then breed the flies and observe how sex-linked traits are passed on from one generation to the next.

Time Required

30 minutes for part A
30 minutes for part B
4 to 6 weeks for part C

white-eyed male

	X^r	Y
red-eyed female X^R	X^RX^r	X^RY
X^R	X^RX^r	X^RY

Figure 1

Punnett square depicting the inheritance of sex-linked traits.

Materials

- 2 varieties of fruit flies, 1 wild-type and 1 breed with an X-linked mutation (such as white eyes or yellow color)
- 3 fruit fly vials and stoppers
- drosophila medium
- water
- small paintbrushes
- index cards
- FlyNap™ or ether for anesthetizing flies
- fly morgue (capped vial filled with isopropyl alcohol)
- magnifying glass or dissecting microscope
- calculator (optional)
- science notebook

Safety Note Avoid inhaling FlyNap™ or ether. Please review and follow the safety guidelines at the beginning of this volume.

Procedure, Part A

1. Practice observing parental flies and sorting them by sex. To do so, anesthesize flies with FlyNap™ or ether and sort males and females on index cards using small paintbrushes. Use caution when handling anesthetized flies so that you do not harm them. Wild-type females have a light-colored abdomen that comes to a point (called the ovipositor) and wild-type males have darker, rounded abdomens as well as sex combs on their front legs (see figure 2 on page 75 of Experiment 12). You may want to use a magnifying lens or dissecting microscope for assistance.

2. Observe the male and female fruit flies of the parental mutant variety. Like the wild-type flies, males and females have different shape abdomens. Mutant males carrying the sex-linked trait will also have very distinctive characteristics that will enable you to distinguish them such as their eye color or body color, aside from their abdomen shape.

3. Put the flies you observed in the morgue. Remove the rest of the the adults in both vials of the parental strains and put them in the morgue. This has to be done because females can store eggs from several mates, so you must use virgin females in the experiment. The hatchlings, which you will use in Procedure 2, will be virgin flies of the pure-bred, parental strains. You will be able to identify the females by their oviposters.

Procedure, Part B

1. Label a mating vial as "F1 generation." The vial will contain medium on which the flies will lay eggs. Prepare the medium by combining one part drosophila medium with one part water. Stir to mix and place in the bottom of a vial. Allow the medium to dry before adding flies and capping with a stopper.

2. Anesthetize and separate the recently hatched males and females from the the stock vials (P generation). (Ideally, this should be done within 8 hours of hatching.)

3. Place four mutant males and four wild-type females into the new mating vial. Label your mating vial as "4 m.m. x 4 w.t.f." Allow the adults to mate and lay eggs for several days to a week.

Procedure, Part C

1. After several days or a week, anesthetize the adults, remove them from the vial, and place them in the morgue.

2. In 8 to 10 days, the flies from the F1 generation will begin to emerge. Create a new breeding vial filled with fresh drosophila medium. Label this vial F1 (first) generation. As they hatch, anesthetize the flies and observe their sex (male or female) and their phenotypes (wild type or mutant). Record this information on the data table.

3. From the emerging flies, place about four males and four newly hatched virgin females into a new breeding vial labeled F2 generation. (Place the remaining flies in the morgue.) Allow them to mate and lay eggs for several days. After that time, the adults should be removed from the vial and placed in the morgue.

4. After the majority of the F2 (second offspring) generation of flies has hatched, generally about 10 days, anesthetize the flies and sort them onto index cards according to their sex and phenotype. Record this data on the data table.

5. At the conclusion of the laboratory, dispose of all flies in the morgue unless otherwise instructed by the teacher.

Data Table				
	Number of wild type males	**Number of mutant males**	**Number of mutant males**	**No. of mutant females**
F1 generation				
F2 generation				

Analysis

1. Draw the Punnett squares that predict the probable outcomes of the first cross between a wild-type female and a mutant male fruit fly and the second cross between the F1 generation males and females.

2. Which phenotype did the flies of the F1 generation express? Can you tell which flies were carrying the mutant gene by their outward appearance?

3. Did your data agree with the predicted ratios from the Punnett squares you created? Why or why not?

4. If you were studying a particular trait, but did not know whether it was sex-linked or autosomal, how could this be determined from your data?

5. Can female fruit flies express sex-linked mutant phenotypes such as the one studied in this lab? Did you observe any females with the trait in this lab? If not, explain why you think that was.

6. Draw a Punnett square predicting the outcome of a cross between the heterozygous (X^RX^r) females and mutant males (X^rY) from the F2 generation. This cross is between a phenotypic wild-type female and a mutant male, just like the first parental cross you performed. How would the lab results be different from the F1 generation in this lab?

What's Going On?

Males express more X-linked traits than females. The reason for this difference is found in the nature of the chromosomes that determine sex. In many species, including humans and fruit flies, females have two X chromosomes, while males have one X and one Y chromosome. The Y chromosome is much smaller than the X chromosome and only carries genes that code for the production of testosterone and male secondary sex characteristics (see Figure 2). The X chromosome, however, carries many genes that affect the phenotype of an individual. If a gene is present on the X chromosome of a male, that gene is always expressed, even if it is recessive, because the Y chromosome does not carry a complimentary gene to override it. However, for a female to express a recessive X-linked trait, she must have two X chromosomes with that recessive allele. If a female has one X chromosome with a dominant trait on it, that trait will be expressed and the recessive allele will be masked. However, that female has a 50 percent chance of passing that recessive allele on to her sons, who will ultimately express that trait. Therefore, recessive alleles on the X chromosome are said to be sex-linked because a much higher number of males than females will express the trait over several generations.

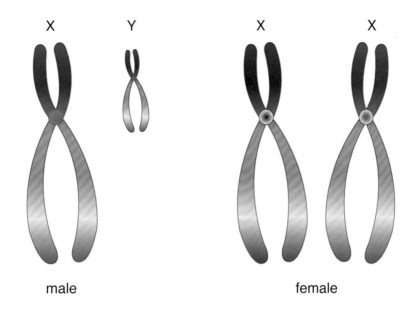

Figure 2

Human sex chromosomes

Connections

Humans and many other species have X and Y sex chromosomes that determine whether they will be male or female. However, in many species, sex is determined differently. For example, in cockroaches and many other types of insects, there is no Y chromosome; males simply have one X chromosome while females have two. In many species of birds, Z and W chromosomes determine sex, and the system is the opposite from the familiar XY system of sex determination. In the ZW system, the male has two of the same type of sex chromosome (ZZ) and the female has two different sex chromosomes (ZW). Insects such as bees and ants have what is known as the *haplodiploid system* of sex determination. All eggs that are fertilized and have two sets of chromosomes are females, and the eggs that are left unfertilized and only have one haploid set of chromosomes are males.

The gender of some organisms is not based on chromosomes. In many species, the sex of an individual is based on the environment in which they live. The temperature at which the eggs are incubated during a critical developmental period determines the sex of most reptiles. Some organisms are capable of changing sexes within their lifetime based on their age or the individuals with whom they interact. Some species of snails, for instance, begin life as males then turn into females later in their life cycle. In species of fish, such as the blue-headed wrasse, all of the fish are females with the exception of the one most dominant individual, which is a male. If that male should die, the next largest female will turn into a male and take on the role of the dominant male in the group. Many other species, including worms, some insects, fish, and snails, do not have different sexes at all. Some individuals are *hermaphrodites* that are capable of producing both egg and sperm in one individual. Others use a system called *parthenogenesis* in which all of the individuals are females who are capable of laying eggs with a full set of chromosomes.

Want to Know More?

See appendix for Our Findings.

Further Reading

O'Neil, Dennis. "Sex-Linked Genes," September 20, 2009. Available online. URL: http://anthro.palomar.edu/biobasis/bio_4.htm. Accessed January 8, 2010. O'Neil's Web site discusses several topics on the biological basis of heredity, including the inheritance of sex-linked traits.

Quinn, Alex. "How Is the Gender of Some Reptiles Determined by Temperature?" *Scientific American*. June 25, 2007. Available online. URL: http://www.scientificamerican.com/article.cfm?id=experts-temperature-sex-determination-reptiles. Accessed January 8, 2010. In this article, Quinn explains some differences between genotypic sex determination and phenotypic sex determination.

"Sex-linked Inheritance Problem Set," Biology Project. Mendelian Genetics. 2009. Available online. URL: http://www.biology.arizona.edu/Mendelian_genetics/problem_sets/sex_linked_inheritance/sex_linked_inheritance.html. Accessed January 8, 2010. This Web site provides tutorials on several topics of genetics including sex-linked traits.

"Virtual Lab: Sex-Linked Traits." Available online. URL: http://www.mhhe.com/biosci/genbio/virtual_labs/BL_15/BL_15.html. Accessed January 8, 2010. This virtual lab lets you cross fruit flies of several varieties to see how traits are passed from parents to offspring.

14. Pedigrees Show Traits Within Families

Topic

Pedigrees show patterns of inheritance that can help determine how a trait is inherited.

Introduction

Geneticists are scientists who study the transmission of genes from parents to their offspring through many generations. The relationships in families and the *phenotypes* of individuals can be studied in a chart called a *pedigree*. Whether studying inheritance in race horses, show dogs, or humans, pedigrees help keep track of the way a trait is passed down from one generation to the next.

Pedigrees are drawn using shapes and lines. Males are represented by squares and females by circles. If an individual expresses a trait, the square or circle is filled. When an individual carries a trait, but does not express it, the shape is half filled. Vertical lines represent generations. A horizontal line connecting a male and female indicates that they are parents. Siblings are shown by shapes attached to vertical lines that are connected by a horizontal line. Figure 1 shows the symbols used in drawing pedigrees.

Humans have 23 pairs of chromosomes, and most genes are found on the *autosomes*, chromosomes 1 through 22. The twenty-third pair of chromosomes is the sex chromosomes, XX in females and XY in males. The X chromosome is larger and carries several other traits unrelated to gender. Traits carried on the X chromosome are described as sex-linked. Very few traits are located on the Y chromosome.

When examining a pedigree, certain patterns may help you understand how a trait is transmitted from one generation to the next. If a trait occurs equally in males and females, it is most likely located on an autosome. A trait that appears in every generation, even if one of the parents does not express the trait, is most likely dominant. A trait that skips generations, or requires two carriers, is probably recessive. Sex-linked traits appear more

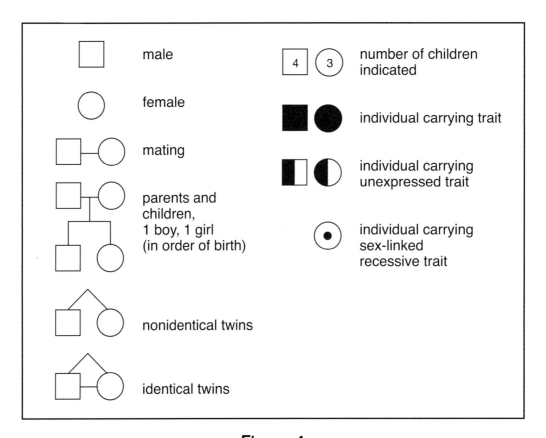

Figure 1
Symbols used to construct pedigrees.

often in males. In this experiment, you will select a trait that interests you and trace its transmission in a family. From the data you gather, you will draw a pedigree.

Time Required

55 minutes in class
1 or 2 days to gather information on family traits

Materials

- access to the Internet or books on genetics
- science notebook

Safety Note   Please review and follow the safety guidelines at the beginning of this volume.

Procedure, Day 1

1. Using the symbols in Figure 1, draw a pedigree of your family, or the family of a friend or neighbor. Include as many individuals and generations as possible.

2. Analyze the individuals in the family for an unusual trait, such as webbed toes or an extra finger, or for the presence of one or more of the traits on the list below (if you are not familiar with them, do research on the Internet or in genetics books):

    a. Attached ear lobes

    b. Hair on the mid digit (middle joint of finger)

    c. Ability to roll the tongue

    d. White forelock

    e. Widow's peak

    f. Dimples

    g. Cleft chin

    h. Color blindness

    i. Hitchhiker's thumb

3. For each individual who has the trait you have selected, fill in the appropriate circle or shape in the pedigree. (If you analyzed more than one trait, you need a pedigree for each trait.)

4. Based on the frequency at which the trait appears, decide whether you think the trait is autosomal dominant, autosomal recessive, or sex-linked.

Analysis

1. Denise and Frank just had their first child, Jasmine. The young parents were surprised to find that their child has sickle cell anemia. Neither Denise nor Frank has the disease, but Frank's aunt and Denise's uncle have it. Draw a pedigree that shows how Jasmine inherited sickle cell anemia.

2. Denise and Frank have a second child, Shawn, who does not have the disease. Add Shawn to the pedigree

3. After Shawn grows up and marries, he wants to know what is the risk that his children will inherit sickle cell anemia. Shawn's wife is Erin. No one in her family has ever had sickle cell disease. Use a Punnett square to show the likelihood that Shawn is a carrier. A

Punnett square is a square divided into four parts that is used to predict the probability that offspring will inherit traits. The mother's genes are written across the top of the box and the father's genes are written on the side. The possible combinations of the parents' genes are filled in the four squares, as shown in the example in Figure 2.

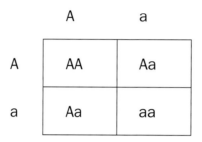

Figure 2

Punnett square

4. If Shawn is a carrier, what is the likelihood that Erin and Shawn's children will inherit the disease?

5. Answer the following questions about the pedigree in Figure 3.

    a. What type of inheritance is shown: autosomal dominant, autosomal recessive, or sex-linked? Explain your reasoning.

    b. What is the relationship of individual 1 in generation III to individual 1 in generation 1?

    c. Individuals 3 and 6 in generation II did not inherit the trait found in individual 1 of generation I. Why not?

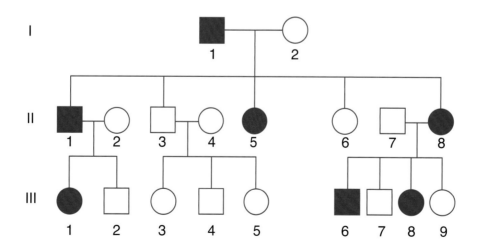

Figure 3

What's Going On?

By studying a pedigree, you can determine the mode of inheritance of a trait. If you traced the characteristic of free earlobes through a family, it most likely appeared in every generation because it is a dominant autosomal trait. A widow's peak, dimples, freckles, tongue rolling, mid-digit hair, and white forelock are also dominant. A cleft chin is a recessive trait, so it may skip one or more generations. Color blindness is a recessive sex-linked trait that most likely appears only in males. The only way a female can inherit color blindness is by getting one allele for the trait from her mother (who could be a carrier with normal vision) and another allele from her father (who would be color blind).

Connections

Several disorders and diseases are described as genetic because they are caused by abnormalities in an individual's genes. Genes code for proteins, large molecules that have many roles. Thousands of different proteins carry out jobs in cells and provide cellular structures. When a gene *mutates,* the protein it produces cannot carry out its function. In many cases, the lack of a functional protein causes a disorder.

More than 6,000 disorders are caused by mutations in single genes. One such condition is cystic fibrosis, an autosomal recessive disease. In individuals with cystic fibrosis, the gene that makes one type of membrane protein is defective. Therefore, this protein does not function. As a result, cells all over the body cannot manage the transport of chloride, causing glands to make an abnormal type of mucus that is unusually thick and sticky. Thick mucus interferes with digestion, resulting in malnutrition, which slows growth. Mucus also clogs the lungs, causes breathing problems and permanent lung damage. The life expectancy for those with this condition is 30 years, and death is most often due to lung disease.

Want to Know More?

See appendix for Our Findings.

Further Reading

"Introduction," Genetic Disorders Detection, 2009. *Merck Manual.* Available online. URL: http://www.merck.com/mmhe/sec22/ch256/

ch256a.html. Accessed January 8, 2010. This Web page discusses the usefulness of genetic counseling for couples at risk of passing on a genetic disease.

McClean, Phillip. "Pedigree Analysis," 2000. Mendelian Genetics. Available online. URL: http://www.ndsu.edu/pubweb/~mcclean/plsc431/mendel/mendel9.htm. Accessed January 8, 2010. McClean explains pedigrees and provides links to other topics related to inheritance in this article.

Tissot, Robert. "Human Genetics for M-1 Students," Available online. URL: http://www.uic.edu/classes/bms/bms655/index.html. Accessed January 8, 2010. The University of Illinois at Chicago provides this Web site for students of basic genetics.

15. Model of a DNA Molecule

Topic

A model of DNA provides insight into the shape and structure of the molecule.

Introduction

The genetic information for each individual is carried in DNA, a macromolecule found in the nucleus of almost every cell. DNA, or deoxyribonucleic acid, contains the genes that code for specific proteins. The actions of these proteins control the activities of the cell.

Structurally, DNA is made up of two strands that are twisted in the shape of a double helix (see Figure 1). Each strand is made up of thousands of subunits called *nucleotides*. A nucleotide has three parts, a sugar, phosphate group, and nitrogenous base. The sugar, deoxyribose, is linked to the phosphate group on one end and a nitrogenous base at the other end. The bases are adenine (A), thymine (T), guanine (G), and cytosine (C). Adenine and guanine are classified as *purines*; the slightly larger thymine and cytosine are *pyrimidines*. Sugar and phosphate make up the backbones of the helix and the nitrogen bases extend into the center. Paired bases are held together by *hydrogen bonds*. Adenine always pairs with thymine and guanine with cytosine. In this experiment, you will demonstrate and analyze the structure of a DNA molecule by building a model.

Time Required

55 minutes

Materials

- access to the Internet or books on DNA
- cardboard

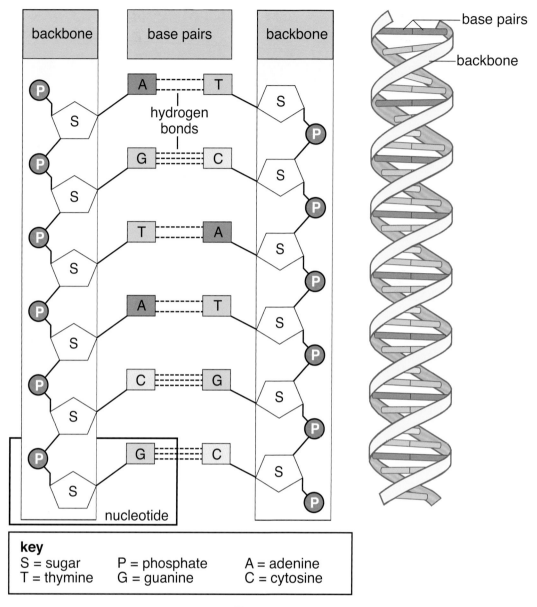

Figure 1

- paper clips
- yarn
- pipe cleaners
- modeling clay
- colored marshmallows
- toothpicks
- jelly beans

- ◈ scissors
- ◈ tape
- ◈ glue
- ◈ photocopy of the grading rubric
- ◈ science notebook

Safety Note **Please review and follow the safety guidelines given at the beginning of this volume.**

Procedure

1. Your job is to design and build a model of a DNA molecule. Your model must include or show the following:
   a. a minimum of 12 pairs of nitrogen bases
   b. a size difference in the purines and pyrimidines
   c. hydrogen bonds holding the bases together
   d. alternating sugars and bases on the sides
   e. a three-dimensional, twisted-ladder shape
   f. a key that explains the parts of the model

2. You can use any of the supplies provided by your teacher, but you will not need to use all of them.

3. As you plan your model, consult the grading rubric on page 97 to be sure you meet all of your teacher's expectations.

4. Before you start building your model, decide what materials you need and how big the model will be. Describe your model and the materials you will use on the data table on page 96. Show your plans and materials list to the teacher. If you get teacher approval, proceed with your model building. If not, modify your work and show it to your teacher again.

5. Once you have teacher approval, assemble the materials you need and begin your work.

6. When you are finished, write your name on the photocopy of the grading rubric and turn it in with the model.

Data Table	
Description of your model	
Your materials list	
Teacher's approval	

Analysis

1. What is DNA?

2. Where is DNA located in your body?

3. A DNA molecule is made up of two strands of nucleotides. What molecules make up one nucleotide?

4. In DNA, why are adenine and thymine paired instead of adenine and guanine?

5. What differentiates the DNA molecules in your cells from the DNA molecules in another student's cells?

Grading Rubric			
Criteria	**3**	**2**	**1**
Model contains bases	12 pairs of bases, each paired correctly	9 to 11 pairs of bases, each paired correctly	8 or fewer bases, each paired correctly
Model shows sugars and phosphates	Sugars and phosphates alternate to form the backbone of each strand; nitrogen bases are attached to sugars.	Sugars and phosphates are represented, but nitrogen bases are not attached to sugars.	Sugars and phosphates are not correctly represented.
Model shows 3D structure	Model is three-dimensional and shows twisted helix.	Model is three-dimensional but not twisted.	Model is not three-dimensional.
Key	The key is present, accurate, and complete.	The key is present, but is not complete *or* not accurate.	The key is present but is neither complete nor accurate.
Neatness	Extremely neat	Fairly neat	Not neat

What's Going On?

Your model shows the basic structure of a DNA molecule. It is likely that the sequence in the bases in your model differs slightly from the sequence in other students' models. In real life, no two individuals, except for identical twins, have exactly the same sequence of bases.

Scientists all over the world contributed bits and pieces of knowledge about DNA to the discovery of its structure. In the 1940s, most scientists believed that DNA carried an individual's genetic information, but they did not know how. Scientists also knew that there were four different nitrogen bases in the molecule. In 1949, the Austrian-American biochemist Erwin

Chargaff (1905–2002) determined that a DNA molecule has the same amounts of adenine and thymine and the same amount of cytosine and guanine. Around the same time in Britain, biophysicst Rosalind Franklin (1920–58) and molecular biologist Maurice Wilkins (1916–2004) were trying to find out exactly what a DNA molecule looked like using *X-ray diffraction*, a technique that exposes molecular crystals to X-ray. In this technique, X-rays bounce off of the crystals and create patterns on X-ray film. By looking at the patterns, Franklin and Wilkins determined that the molecule is a double helix.

During the same time period, American molecular biologist James Watson (1928–) and British molecular biologist Francis Crick (1916–2004) were working on a similar project, but using slightly different techniques. They were building stick and ball models of DNA. In 1953, Watson and Crick put together all of the information available and came up with a model that explained everything scientists knew about DNA. The two scientists were awarded the Nobel Prize for their work in 1962.

Connections

The double helix structure of DNA and the specific pattern of bases suggested to scientists a mechanism for replication. During cell division, a DNA molecule opens or "unzips" so that it forms two separate strands. When unzipped, the bases within DNA are exposed. Free nucleotides base pair with the exposed bases, forming exact copies of both strands. Each new molecule is made up of one of the original strands and one new strand (see Figure 2). After replication, the nucleus contains two identical, double-stranded molecules of genetic information. When the cell divides, each new cell gets one of the copies.

Want to Know More?

See appendix for Our Findings.

Further Reading

Learn.Genetics. "Build a DNA Molecule," 2010. Available online. URL: http://learn.genetics.utah.edu/content/begin/dna/builddna/. Accessed January 9, 2010. This interactive Web page demonstrates the structure of a DNA molecules.

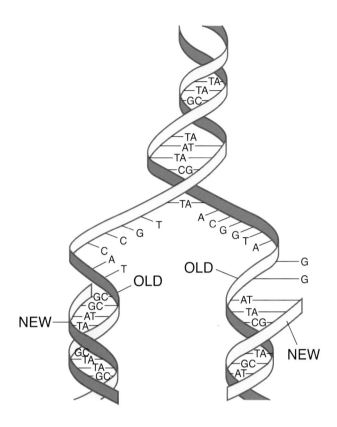

Figure 2

DNA replication

Nobelprize.org. "The Discovery of the Molecular Structure of DNA—The Double Helix," 2010. Available online. URL: http://nobelprize.org/educational_games/medicine/dna_double_helix/readmore.html. Accessed January 9, 2010. This Web site reviews the discoveries that led to our current understanding of DNA's structure.

Wright, Pearce. "Erwin Chargaff," July 2, 2002. *Guardian*. Available online. URL: http://www.guardian.co.uk/news/2002/jul/02/guardianobituaries.obituaries. Accessed January 9, 2010. Wright's obituary of Chargaff points out the scientist's contributions to the elucidation of DNA's structure and function.

16. Introduction to Gel Electrophoresis

Topic

Techniques for separating molecules in gel electrophoresis can be practiced using dyes.

Introduction

You probably know that DNA, the nuclear material that carries genetic information, is located in the nuclei of cells. To analyze a sample of DNA, scientists use *gel electrophoresis*, a method of separating the fragments of molecules by size as they travel through a gel. The same technique can be used to separate other molecules, such as proteins. In gel electrophoresis, samples are loaded into an agarose gel, a sheet of congealed material that lies in an electrophoresis chamber (Figure 1). The gel is covered in a buffer solution that conducts an electrical current. Then electrodes are connected to both ends of the electrophoresis chamber, and a small electric current is applied. This creates a negative pole and a positive pole in the gel. Negatively charged molecules migrate through the gel toward the positive pole. Positively charged molecules travel toward the negative pole. Small molecules can travel faster than large ones, so they travel the furthest. In this way, the fragments are separated and can be analyzed. In this experiment, you will learn more about gel electrophoresis by separating the components of dyes.

Time Required

55 minutes

Materials

- microtubes containing 20 microliters (µL) of the following dyes:
  - ✔ bromophenol blue
  - ✔ Janus green

✔ orange G

✔ safranin O

✔ xylene cyanol

✔ unknown dye

◆ micropipettor (1 to 20μL)

◆ pipette tips

◆ electrophoresis chamber

◆ power unit for electrophoresis chamber

◆ melted 0.8 percent agarose in flask (in hot water bath), about 30 milliliters (ml)

◆ 1X TBE Tris-borate-EDTA solution (TBE) (about 100 ml, enough to fill electrophoresis unit)

◆ metric ruler

◆ hot mitts

◆ science notebook

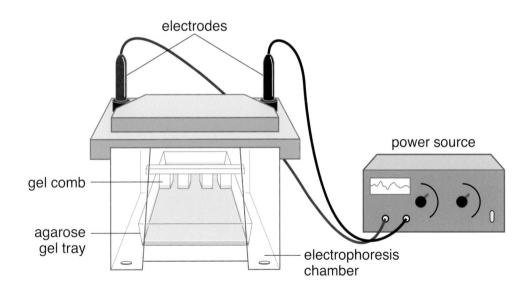

Figure 1

The complete agarose electrophoresis chamber is made up of many parts including electrodes, gel comb, and gel tray. The only other item you need is a power source.

| Safety Note | Take care when working with electrical devices. Please review and follow the safety guidelines at the beginning of this volume. |

Procedure

1. Secure the dams to the ends of the gel tray of the electrophoresis chamber to prevent hot agarose from running into the electrophoresis chamber. If your tray is not equipped with dams, tape the ends of the tray as shown in Figure 2b.

2. Using hot mitts to hold the flask, pour the melted agarose into the gel tray (see Figure 2b).

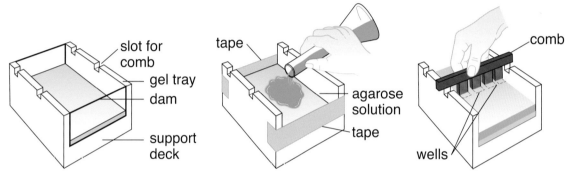

a. Secure dams to gel tray.

b. Add agarose solution to tray.

c. Place comb in center of tray to make wells

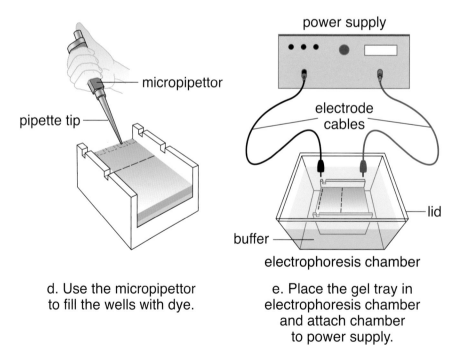

d. Use the micropipettor to fill the wells with dye.

e. Place the gel tray in electrophoresis chamber and attach chamber to power supply.

Figure 2

3. Place the comb in the center slots of the electrophoresis tray (see Figure 2c).

4. Let the tray of agarose gel cool for about 10 minutes (min).

5. When the agarose gel is cool, gently remove the comb and the dams or tape.

6. Put a pipette tip on the micropipettor. Using the micropipettor, transfer a 10 µL of bromthymol blue dye into the first well in the agarose gel. To do so, gently place the pipette tip into the well and release the dye (see Figure 2d).

7. Put a new tip on the micropipettor.

8. Repeat steps 6 through 7 for each of the four remaining known dyes and for the unknown dye.

9. In your science notebook, draw a sketch of the gel chamber and label the sketch to show the position of each dye sample and the unknown dye.

10. Place the gel tray in the electrophoresis chamber.

11. Pour TBE over the gel so that the gel tray is completely covered. Put a cover on the chamber.

12. Connect the chamber electrodes to the power supply, and plug the power supply (see Figure 2e).

13. Run the gel for about 45 min.

14. Unplug the power supply. Remove the electrodes from the gel chamber. Remove the top of the chamber.

15. Remove the gel tray and place it on paper towels on your desktop. Use the ruler to measure the distances in millimeters (mm) from the wells to each band of color. Record the distances in your science notebook.

Analysis

1. What do you think is the purpose of the TBE buffer?

2. Which dyes moved toward the positive pole? Which ones moved toward the negative pole?

3. Based on your observations, what is the electrical charge of bromthymol blue? What is the electrical charge of janus green?

4. The dye that migrated the greatest distance is made of the smallest molecules. Which dye is this? How far did it migrate?

5. Compare the bands of the unknown dye to those of the known dyes. What does the unknown dye contain?

What's Going On?

In this experiment, you separated the components of several dyes and compared them to an unknown dye. By doing so, you saw how a gel electrophoresis chamber is set up and learned how molecules are separated by size and electrical charge. The techniques used in preparing the gel, using the buffer solution, and setting up the gel chambers are very similar to those used in separating DNA fragments. One important difference is in the placement of the comb that created the wells. In this experiment, you positioned the comb in the middle of the gel. This was done so that you could observe that some dyes move toward the positive pole and others toward the negative pole. Since opposite charges attract, you can determine the electrical charges on the dyes. In this experiment, orange G, xylene cyanol, and bromthymol blue moved toward the positive pole. Safranin O and Janus green moved toward the negative pole because they are positively charged dyes. The small molecules traveled through the gel faster than the large ones. In this experiment, orange G is the smallest molecule.

Connections

Agarose is an extract of agar, a polymer taken from seaweed. Because agar has a thickening quality, it is also used in food like ice cream and in products such as shampoo and conditioner. When mixed with water, agar forms a gel that is similar in consistency to Jell-O™, but it does not soften when it gets warm. The particles in an agarose gel act like an obstacle course for the molecules traveling through the gel. Small particles can get through the obstacle course more easily than large ones. To visualize this, imagine that you and some friends are going to run from one side of a wooded park to the other. If all of you hold hands and run across the park, your progress will be slow as you negotiate the group through the trees. However, if you cross the park as individuals, you will get to the other side quickly and easily.

 **Want to Know More?**

See appendix for Our Findings.

Further Reading

Biotechnology and Genetic Engineering. "Principles of Gel Electrophoresis," January 3, 2000. Available online. URL: http://www.vivo. colostate.edu/hbooks/genetics/biotech/gels/principles.html. Accessed January 20, 2010. This Web site provides information on electrophoresis science and explains the uses of different types of gels.

Dolan Learning Center. "Biology Animation Center, Gel Electrophoresis." Available online. URL: http://www.dnalc.org/resources/animations/ gelelectrophoresis.html. Accessed January 24, 2010. Cold Springs Harbor Laboratory provides an animation that explains the structure of DNA and how to separate DNA fragments in gel electrophoresis.

Learn.Genetics. "Gel Electrophoresis Virtual Lab," 2010. Available online. URL: http://learn.genetics.utah.edu/content/labs/gel/. Accessed January 20, 2010. Students can sort molecules, load them in to a virtual gel, and measure their progress in this virtual experiment on gel electrophoresis.

17. DNA Gel Electrophoresis

Topic

DNA fragments that are cut with restriction enzymes can be separated using gel electrophoresis.

Introduction

DNA, the genetic material in the nuclei of cells, is a long molecule. To analyze an individual's DNA, scientists cut it into fragments of different lengths, then separate the fragments using *gel electrophoresis*. The chemicals used to cut DNA are *restriction enzymes*. Usually, more than one type of restriction enzyme is used. Each type recognizes and binds to specific sequences of nucleotides on the double-strand molecule. For example, the restriction enzyme EcoR1 recognizes the sequence:

GAATTC

CTTAAG

This enzyme cuts between the G and A on the top strand and the A and G on the bottom strand (see Figure 1). Another restriction enzyme, Sma1, recognizes the sequence:

CCCGGG

GGGCCC

It cuts between the C and G on both strands.

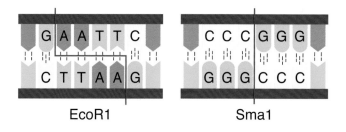

Figure 1

Restriction enzymes make cuts at specific nucleotide sequences.

Once DNA is cut into pieces, the fragments are loaded into an *agarose gel* and placed in an electrophoresis chamber (see Figure 1 on page 101 of Experiment 16). Because DNA is negatively charged, all of the fragments migrate toward the positive pole. The sizes of the fragments determine how quickly they move. Large fragments move very slowly and therefore do not travel very far along the length of the gel. Small fragments can travel faster and cover a longer distance. In this experiment, you will carry out gel electrophoresis using DNA that you cut with restriction enzymes.

Time Required

45 minutes on day 1
45 minutes on day 2
45 minutes on day 3

Materials

- microtubes containing the following labeled samples:

  Microtube 1—Uncut DNA

  Microtube 2—*Hind*III

  Microtube 3—*Bam*HI

  Microtube 4—*Eco*R1

  Microtube X—Unknown

- micropipettor (1 to 20 microliters [µL])

- pipette tips

- ice bath

- 60 milliliters (ml) methylene blue stain

- staining tray

- light box

- electrophoresis chamber

- loading dye

- distilled water

- power unit for electrophoresis chamber

- melted 0.8 percent agarose in flask (in hot water bath), about 30 ml

- 1X TBE Tris-borate/EDTA solution (TBE) (about 100 ml, enough to fill electrophoresis unit)
- metric ruler
- hot mitts
- roll of plastic wrap
- gloves
- access to a refrigerator
- science notebook

Safety Note Take care when working with electrical devices. Methylene blue may permanently stain clothing. Please review and follow the safety guidelines at the beginning of this volume.

Procedure, Day 1

1. Put a pipette tip on the micropipettor and set the micropipettor for 1 µL. Transfer 1 µL of TBE solution into each microtube.

2. Transfer 8 µL of DNA into microtube 2. Deposit the DNA on the inside of the tube.

3. Gently knock the tube several times to mix the contents. Tap the microtube on the desktop a few time to move all the contents to the bottom of the microtube.

4. Repeat steps 2 and 3 to transfer DNA into microtubes 3, 4, and X.

5. Reset the micropipettor to 10 µL. Transfer 10 µL of DNA to microtube 1.

6. Incubate the DNA by placing the microtubes in a 37 degree Celsus (°C) water bath for 45 minutes (min). After incubation, store the tubes in the refrigerator until the next class period.

7. While the tubes are incubating, prepare the gel. Secure the dams to the ends of the gel tray to prevent hot agarose from running into the electrophoresis chamber. If your gel tray does not have dams, wrap tape around the ends of the gel tray.

8. Using hot mitts to hold the flask, pour the melted agarose into the gel tray.

9. Place the comb at one end of the electrophoresis tray.

10. Let the tray of agarose gel cool for about 10 min.

11. When the agarose gel is cool, gently remove the comb and the dams or tape.

12. Cover the gel in plastic wrap and refrigerate overnight.

Procedure, Day 2

1. Add 1 µL of loading dye to each microtube. Use a new micropipette tip for each microtube. Gently knock the tubes several times to mix the contents. Tap the tubes on the desktop a few time to move all the contents to the bottom of the tube.

2. Set the micropipettor to 10 µL. Transfer 10 µL of Sample 1 (from microtube 1) into the first well (see Figure 2). To do so, place your elbows on the table, carefully lower the micropipettor tip into the first well, and depress the plunger. Be careful to avoid jabbing the tip through the gel.

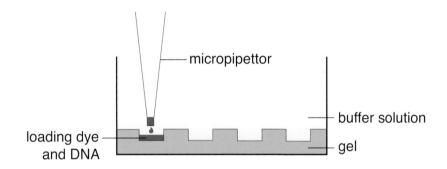

Figure 2

3. Put a new tip on the micropipettor and repeat step 2 for the other microtubes and wells.

4. In your science notebook, draw a sketch of the gel chamber and write down the positions of DNA with restrictive enzymes.

5. Pour TBE over the gel so that the gel tray is completely covered.

6. Place the cover on the electrophoresis chamber. Connect the chamber electrodes to the power supply, and plug in the power supply.

7. Run the gel for 45 to 60 min or until the first band (loading dye) is about 1 centimeter (cm) from the end of the gel.

8. Unplug the power supply. Remove the electrodes from the gel chamber. Remove the cover from the electrophoresis chamber.

9. Remove the liquid from the electrophoresis chamber. Take out the gel tray and gently push the gel into a staining tray.

10. Put on a pair of gloves. Pour 60 mL of methylene blue stain over the gel. Cover the gel with plastic wrap and let it sit overnight.

Procedure, Day 3

1. Pour the stain off of the gel into a container provided by your teacher.

2. Pour enough distilled water over the gel to cover. Let the gel sit in the water for about 10 min. Pour out the water.

3. Gently transfer the stained gel to a light box. (Be careful; the gel is fragile and will break easily.)

4. Draw a picture of your stained gel showing the locations of the bands of DNA.

5. Measure the distance of each band from the well. (Measure from the inner edge of the well to the front edge of the band.) Record the data in your science notebook.

6. The relative mobility, or the R_f, of each fragment can be used to determine the number of base pairs in that fragment. Calculate the R_f in millimeters (mm) of each fragment using the formula:

$$R_f = \frac{\text{distance the DNA fragment traveled in mm}}{\text{distance in mm from the well to the band of dye}}$$

Analysis

1. Why do the banding patterns in microtubes 2 and 3 look different?
2. Which two samples have the same banding pattern?
3. What enzyme was used in microtube X? How do you know?
4. Why would a scientist want to know the R_f of a DNA fragment?

What's Going On?

In this procedure, you prepared an agarose gel with the wells at one end. DNA has a negative charge, so all of the fragments traveled toward the positive pole. Because the DNA samples were cut with different enzymes, the fragments produced were of various sizes. Small fragments traveled further through the gel than large ones. Staining revealed the location of the DNA bands. The only two samples that were the same were in microtubes 3 and X. These two DNA samples had been cut with the same restriction enzymes, *Bam*HI.

The negative charge in DNA comes from its phosphate groups. DNA is made of two long chains of nucleotides twisted to form a double helix. Each nucleotide is made up of a nitrogenous base, the sugar deoxyribose, and a negatively charged phosphate group. Alternating sugar and phosphate groups make up the backbone of a DNA molecule and nucleotides extend into the center of the helix. The arrangement of the nucleotides creates a code that carries genetic information.

Connections

Even though every person has his or her own, distinctive DNA, only one-tenth of 1 percent of the molecule is unique. To use DNA to identify an individual, scientists must focus on that critical distinctive portion. To do so, DNA is digested with restriction enzymes that only recognize sequences in the unique regions. This technique, known as *restriction fragment length polymorphism (RFLP),* is effective because the presence or absence of certain recognition sites produces fragments of varying lengths. These fragments can be separated by electrophoresis for identification purposes.

To carry out RFLP, the scientist must have a large sample of DNA. In addition, the sample must be relatively new or well-preserved so that it has not been degraded. Polymerase chain reaction (PCR) is a newer procedure that takes a small sample of DNA and makes millions of copies of it. This form of DNA amplification provides scientists with larger samples that can then be analyzed with RFLP or other techniques.

Want to Know More?

See appendix for Our Findings.

Further Reading

"Gel Electrophoresis and DNA Technology," 2008. Molecular Station. Available online. URL: http://www.molecularstation.com/dna/dna-gelelectrophoresis/. Accessed January 20, 2010. This article explains the basic technique of electrophoresis and discusses its uses.

Human Genome Project Information. "DNA Forensics," June 16, 2009. Available online. URL: http://www.ornl.gov/sci/techresources/Human_ Genome/elsi/forensics.shtml#3. Accessed January 24, 2010. This Web site explains how DNA is analyzed by forensic scientists and provides links to other relevant sites.

"Recombinant DNA Technology." Kenyon College, Biology Department. Available online. URL: http://biology.kenyon.edu/courses/biol114/ Chap08/Chapter_08a.html. Accessed January 24, 2010. This Web site explains how gel electrophoresis is done and discusses its relationship to research in recombinant DNA.

18. Control of Gene Expression

Topic

A model of the *operon* that controls the breakdown of lactose can show how gene expression is controlled.

Introduction

A *gene* is a section of DNA on a chromosome that codes for a protein. When a gene is activated or expressed, *transcription* occurs and the message on DNA is converted to messenger RNA (mRNA). The process requires an enzyme, *RNA polymerase*. Messenger RNA moves to the cytoplasm and attaches to a *ribosome* where it directs the assembly of amino acids to form a protein, a process called *translation*.

Every cell contains the same set of chromosomes with the same genes. However, all cells do not need to manufacture all proteins. For example, cells in the pancreas make the protein *insulin*, but skin and muscle cells do not. This is possible because genes can be "turned on" or "turned off." Insight into gene expression came from research on the DNA of *Escherichia coli* (*E. coli*), bacterial residents of the human digestive tract. *E. coli* can break down lactose, a sugar found in milk. Lactose is a disaccharide made up of two monosaccharides, glucose and galactose. When we drink milk, lactose stimulates *E. coli* to make the enzymes needed to break it down. The production of these enzymes depends on three factors: structural genes, the *promoter*, and the *operator*. Structural genes make the enzymes needed to digest lactose. The promoter is a section of DNA that recognizes RNA polymerase and activates it to begin *transcription*, the process in which the DNA code is copied to a strand of mRNA. This process requires RNA polymerase. Once transcribed, mRNA moves to the cytoplasm where it directs the production of *lactase* and other milk-digesting enzymes. The operator is a segment of DNA that binds to an inhibitory protein that prevents transcription and therefore production of the enzymes. These three factors work together as an operon that controls production of a protein. The operon that controls the breakdown of lactose is named the *lac operon.* In this experiment, you will make a model of the lac operon.

Time Required

45 minutes

Materials

- craft (Popsicle™) stick
- modeling clay or Play-Doh™ in 3 colors
- red, blue, and green markers
- black pen
- science notebook

Safety Note   Please review and follow the safety guidelines at the beginning of this volume.

Procedure

1. Make a model of the lac operon using a craft stick. To do so:

   a. Using Figure 1 as a guide, use a blue marker to draw the three structural genes on the craft stick. (Althought the actual lac operon curves, your craft stick model will be straight.) Use the black pen to label the genes "z," "y," and "a."

   b. Use a green marker to draw the operator section. Use the black pen to label this region "operator."

   c. Use a red marker to draw the promoter. Label the area "promoter" with the black pen.

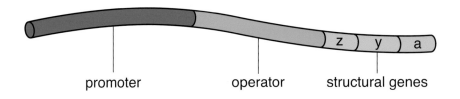

Figure 1

2. Roll a piece of clay or Play-Doh™ into a flattened ball. This ball represents RNA polymerase.

3. Roll a second piece of clay or Play-Doh™ of a different color into a small U-shape. This represents a repressor molecule.

4. Roll a third piece of clay or Play-Doh™ of another color into a small ball that will fit inside the U-shaped repressor molecule. This represents lactose, the inducer.

5. Position the repressor molecule on the operator to model turning off the operon (see Figure 2). Notice that with the repressor molecule in place, polymerase cannot bind to and slide along the length of the operon.

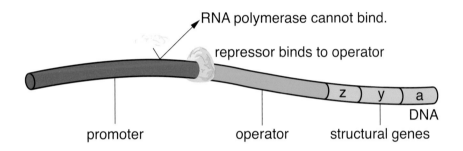

Figure 2

6. Remove the repressor molecule. Place lactose, the inducer, inside the repressor.

7. Place RNA polymerase on the operator. Slide the molecule along the length of the operon (see Figure 3).

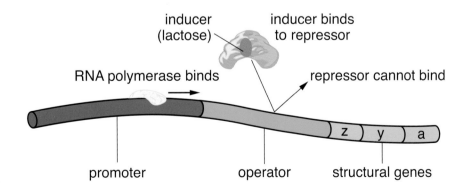

Figure 3

Analysis

1. What is transcription?

2. When the repressor is in place, can RNA polymerase slide down the operon and bind to the operator? Explain your answer.

3. Can the repressor molecule bind to DNA when the inducer is attached to it? Explain your answer.

4. After the inducer binds with the repressor, is anything present to prevent RNA polymerase from moving along the operon?

5. What process can occur if RNA polymerase is present?

6. In your own words, explain how the presence of lactose causes the production of lactose-digesting enzymes.

What's Going On?

In this experiment, you used a model to understand how the expression of the structural genes that make enzymes for the digestion of lactose is controlled. The presence of lactose is the trigger for producing the enzymes. Normally a repressor protein sits on the section of DNA that controls production of lactose-digesting enzymes. When lactose is present, it binds to the repressor protein, removes it from the DNA, and enables RNA polymerase to begin the process of transcription. This is a type of negative control, so named because the process of transcription is always blocked unless lactose molecules are present. In this case, the presence of lactose signals the cell to break down the molecule.

Connections

The first operons were studied in bacteria because they are simple cells compared to those in humans and many other organisms. Most of the operons in bacteria act as switches that either turn on or turn off the production of an enzyme. However, gene control in multicellular organisms is complex. *Transcription factors* are groups of proteins that bind to specific sections of DNA and begin transcription. These factors are put into motion by chemical signals. Since transcription factors are proteins, they are encoded on DNA. In some cases, segments of transcription factor genes are physically near the genes they control. In other cases, this is not so. However, DNA can form loops that bring the transcription factor genes close to the genes they regulate.

Want to Know More?

See appendix for Our Findings.

Further Reading

Billiet, Paul. "The Lac Operon," 2007. Available online. URL: http://www.saburchill.com/IBbiology/chapters03/images/08_lac_OPERON.ppt#256,1,THElacOPERON. Accessed January 24, 2010. In this PowerPoint presentation, Billiet discusses the details of lac operon function, including the role of the regulatory gene.

"The Lac Operon." Sumanas Inc., Animated Tutorials. Available online. URL: http://www.sumanasinc.com/webcontent/animations/content/lacoperon.html. Accessed January 24, 2010. This animation explains the components of the lac operon and shows how those components interact.

"The Lactose Paradigm." Dartmouth College. Available online. URL: http://www.dartmouth.edu/~cbbc/courses/movies/LacOperon.html. Accessed January 24, 2010. This video demonstrates and explains the mechanism of the lac operon.

19. Genetics Learning Centers

Topic

Genetic traits are transmitted from parents to offspring through several modes of inheritance.

Introduction

Geneticists are scientists who study the manner in which traits are passed from one generation to another. Traits are controlled by *genes*, sections of *chromosomes* that code for specific characteristics. Humans have 23 pairs of chromosomes (see Figure 1), one pair of sex chromosomes, which determine if an individual is male or female, and 22 pairs of *autosomes,* which carry the majority of genes.

There are several important modes of inheritance, or ways in which traits are inherited. Some traits are *autosomal dominant*, meaning that they are carried on autosomes and that they mask the presence of *recessive traits*.

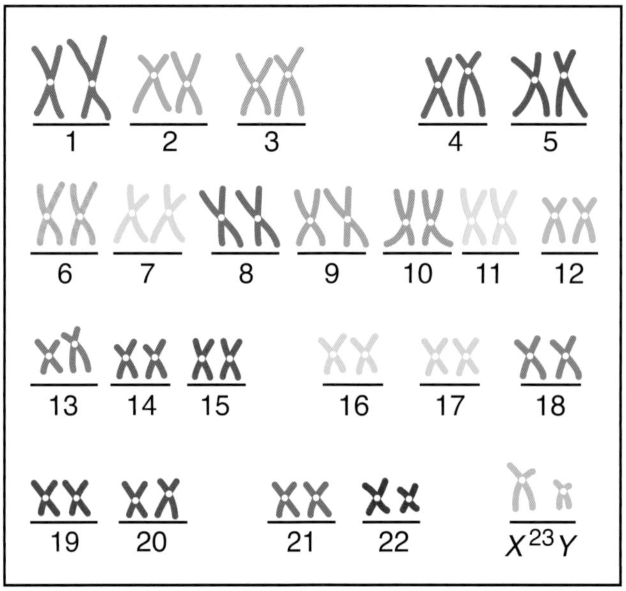

Figure 1

Humans have 23 pairs of chromosomes.

Traits that are *autosomal recessive* do not show up if the dominant gene is present. Some traits are *codominant* because there are two different versions of the gene and they are both expressed. In this situation, both versions influence the expression of the trait. Traits that are X-linked dominant are carried on the X chromosome, the larger of the two sex chromosomes. These traits can occur in both males and females. X-linked recessive traits appear more frequently in males. Mitochondrial inheritance refers to traits that are passed from mothers to offspring. These traits are carried on *mitochondrial DNA*, the genetic information carried within a woman's mitochondria, the organelles that are responsible for converting sugar to usable energy. In this activity, you will conduct research on the mode of inheritance assigned to you by your teacher and use your expertise to construct a learning center that the entire class can enjoy.

Time Required

55 minutes for part A
two 55-minute periods for part B
55 minutes for part C

Materials

- ⇨ access to the Internet or books on genetics
- ⇨ printer (optional)
- ⇨ art supplies (such as cardboard, construction paper, paint, glue, markers, tape, papier-mâché, yarn, and clay)
- ⇨ ruler
- ⇨ scissors
- ⇨ cardboard box
- ⇨ trifold display board
- ⇨ several photocopies of the assessment rubric
- ⇨ science notebook

Safety Note   Take care when working with scissors or other sharp tools. Please review and follow the safety guidelines at the beginning of this volume.

Procedure, Part A

1. Working in groups of three or four, use the Internet or books on genetics to research the mode of inheritance assigned to you by your teacher. Learn all you can about the topic. The modes of inheritance include the following:

    > Autosomal dominant
    >
    > Autosomal recessive
    >
    > Codominance
    >
    > X-linked dominant
    >
    > X-linked recessive
    >
    > Mitochondrial

    In your research, be sure to write down details about how traits are passed from parents to offspring and examples of traits inherited in this manner. Record your findings in your science notebook.

2. Sketch, trace, or print two or more pictures that help explain the topic you have been assigned.

Procedure, Part B

1. Working with your group, create a display that will act as a learning center for your classmates. Your learning center should be interesting and attractive and provide accurate, educational material. All of the required information must be displayed in a way that other students can study. Students will use your display to answer the Analysis questions.

2. The assessment rubric shows the required material for the learning station and the points you can earn by meeting each requirement. Examine this rubric closely before you begin making your learning center. Notice that your learning center must include:

    a. a written explanation of the mode of inheritance.

    b. lists of traits, diseases, or conditions that relate to this topic.

    c. descriptions of the most common diseases or conditions associated with the mode of inheritance.

    d. a Punnett square showing the mode of inheritance.

    e. a pedigree showing the mode of inheritance.

    f. a vocabulary activity for your classmates.

3. Read the Analysis questions before you begin work on your center. Make sure that your learning center answers all of the Analysis questions that are relevant to the mode of inheritance that you are researching.

Assessment Rubric

Names of Group Members_____

_____

Name of Topic_____

Requirements	Points Possible	Points Earned
Written description (minimum 200 words) of the mode of inheritance	15	
List of traits (or diseases or conditions) that are passed on through this mode of inheritance	15	
Description of diseases or conditions	15	
Punnett square showing this mode of inheritance	15	
Pedigree showing this mode of inheritance	15	
Vocabulary activity that contains at least 15 terms that are important to your mode of inheritance. Examples of vocabulary activities are puzzles, Frayer diagrams, and matching activities.	15	
Display is attractive	5	
Display is neat	5	
Total	100	

Procedure, Part C

1. Visit each mode of inheritance learning center to carry out peer assessments. Use a photocopy of the rubric to assess each station. When you have completed your assessment, give the rubrics to the teacher.

2. Visit each mode of inheritance learning center as a learner. Read the information provided, study the pictures, and complete the vocabulary activity.

3. Answer the Analysis questions.

Analysis

1. Match each description to a mode of inheritance. (Modes of inheritance may be used more than once. Not all modes of inheritance are used.)

   Modes of inheritance:

   autosomal dominant   autosomal recessive   codominant
   X-linked dominant   X-linked recessive   mitochondrial

   a. Fathers cannot pass the traits to their sons.

   b. A person with the trait usually has at least one affected parent.

   c. A person with the trait may have two unaffected parents.

   d. All daughters of an affected male and a normal female will show the trait.

   e. Only mothers pass traits to their offspring.

   f. Males inherit the trait more frequently than females.

   g. The trait occurs in every generation of a family.

2. Name the mode of inheritance that is responsible for each of the following traits, diseases, or conditions. (Not all modes of inheritance will be used.)

   a. Fragile X syndrome

   b. ABO blood groups

   c. Cystic fibrosis

   d. Huntington's disease

3. Name the mode of inheritance shown in each of the pedigrees in Figure 2. (Not all modes of inheritance will be used.)

a.

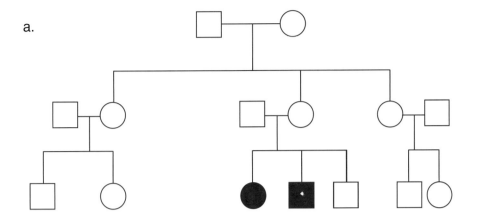

b.

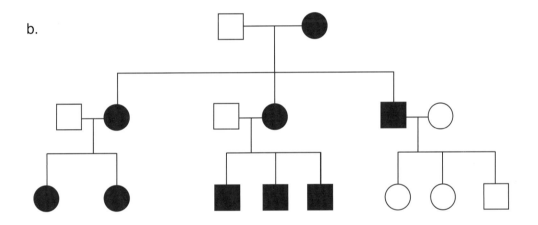

c.

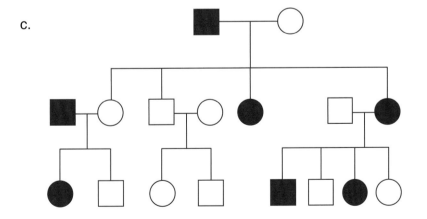

Figure 2

What's Going On?

A pedigree can tell a geneticist a lot about traits and how they are inherited. One of the easiest patterns to recognize is one that shows the inheritance of an autosomal dominant trait. In this type of inheritance, every individual carrying the trait has a parent carrying the trait, males and females are equally affected, and the trait appears in every generation. Some of the diseases that are inherited in this manner include Huntington's disease, a disorder that causes the wasting away of nerve cells, and neurofibromatosis, in which nerve tissue grows tumors. In the inheritance of autosomal recessive traits, individuals expressing the trait have parents who do not. The parents are *heterozygotes*, meaning that they carry the recessive gene, but they have a dominant gene that prevents its expression. Diseases transmitted as autosomal recessive traits include cystic fibrosis which leads to production of thick mucus in the lungs and digestive system, and Tay-Sachs disease which causes degeneration of brain cells.

X-linked dominant traits are carried on the X chromosome. Pedigrees showing this type of inheritance reveal that the affected traits are found in males and females, although females are more frequently affected. Fathers cannot pass traits to sons in this type of inheritance. Diseases include fragile X syndrome, a cause of mental retardation, and Coffin-Lowry syndrome, which leads to skeletal abnormalities.

X-linked recessive traits are also carried on the X chromosomes. In a pedigree, traits show up more often in males, and transmission never occurs from male to male. However, women can be carriers and pass the trait to sons. X-linked recessive diseases include hemophilia, a bleeding disorder, and duchenne muscular dystrophy, a muscle wasting disorder.

In codominant inheritance, there are two versions of a gene and both are expressed. One is not dominant over the other. Blood type is determined by codominance. One of the few codominant diseases is Alpha-1 Antitrypsin Deficiency, which is associated with liver and lung disease.

Mitochondrial, or maternal, inheritance can be explained by the manner in which *fertilization* occurs. When egg and sperm fuse, only the DNA of the sperm enters the egg. The tail and *midpiece*, which carries mitochondria, drop off (see Figure 2). Therefore, the embryo receives only mitochondrial DNA from the mother. Traits carried on mitochondrial DNA are passed on by the mother and appear in every generation in both males and females. One genetic disease transmitted by this mode of inheritance is Leber

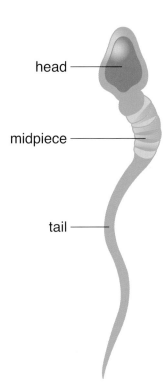

Figure 2

Sperm

hereditary optic neuropathy, in which nerve cells in the eye degenerate and result in loss of vision.

Connections

Human blood groups are determined by three versions or *alleles* of a gene, A, B, and O. A and B are both dominant alleles and O is recessive. If an individual inherits A from one parent and B from the other, his or her blood type is AB. A person who inherits A and O will have type A blood. Similarly, an individual who inherits B and O will have type B blood. To have type O blood, one must inherit O from both parents.

On the cellular level, an individual with type A blood has proteins called A *antigens* on their red blood cells. These people produce *antibodies* to B blood, which would cause clumping to occur if they were given B blood. Those with type B blood have B antigens and produce antibodies to type A blood, so they cannot receive type A. People with AB blood have both types of antigens and do not produce any antibodies. These individuals are universal recipients since they can receive blood from anyone. Individuals with O blood lack either type of antigen and produces antibodies to both and are described as universal donors.

Want to Know More?

See appendix for Our Findings.

Further Reading

O'Neil, Dennis. "Sex-Linked Genes," *Biological Basis of Heredity: An Introduction to Basic Cell Structures Related to Genetic Inheritance*. 2010. Available online. URL: http://anthro.palomar.edu/biobasis/bio_4.htm. Accessed January 23, 2010. O'Neil does an excellent job of explaining how traits on sex chromosomes are transmitted in this chapter of an Web tutorial.

"Pedigrees and Modes of Inheritance," *Biology Encyclopedia*, 2010. Available online. URL: http://www.biologyreference.com/Oc-Ph/Pedigrees-and-Modes-of-Inheritance.html. Accessed January 23, 2010. This Web site explains how autosomal dominant, autosomal recessive, and X-linked traits are passed from parents to offspring.

"What Are the Different Ways in Which a Genetic Condition Can Be Inherited?" *Genetics Home Reference*. January 18, 2010. Available online. URL: http://ghr.nlm.nih.gov/handbook/inheritance/inheritancepatterns. Accessed January 23, 2010. This Web site gives examples of disease conditions and explains how they are inherited.

20. Genetic Engineering Presentation

Topic

Genetic engineering has made it possible to develop technology in agriculture and medicine.

Introduction

Genetic engineering is a technique for altering the DNA within an organism. DNA forms chromosomes, structures in the nuclei of cells that carry genetic information. Scientists use a *restriction enzyme*, a chemical that can cut a strand of DNA, to remove a *gene* from its normal location. Then they insert the gene into the DNA of another organism.

Some of the earliest work in genetic engineering moved human genes into bacterial DNA to yield products that could be used as medications. Using similar techniques, scientists can also transfer a fragment of DNA carrying a desirable trait into other types of organisms. For example, a gene for insect resistance can be removed from *Bacillus thuringiensis* (Bt), a type of bacterium that produces insect toxin, and transferred to a plant (see Figure 1). As a result, insects do not feed on the plant. Many crops, especially corn and soybeans, currently carry genes for insect resistance. Others crops plants carry genes that make them resistant to *herbicides*, chemicals that kill weeds. Farmers can spray their entire fields with herbicide without worrying about damaging their crops.

In this activity, you and your laboratory partner(s) will conduct research on various projects that involve genetic engineering. You will present the information you find to the class.

Time Required

three or four 55-minute class periods

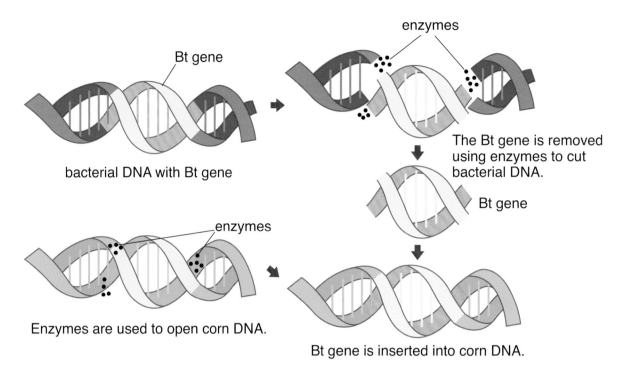

enzymes

Bt gene

bacterial DNA with Bt gene

The Bt gene is removed using enzymes to cut bacterial DNA.

Bt gene

enzymes

Enzymes are used to open corn DNA.

Bt gene is inserted into corn DNA.

Figure 1

The Bt gene is added to corn to make the corn insect-resistant.

Materials

- ○◇ access to the Internet or books on genetic engineering
- ○◇ printer (optional)
- ○◇ materials to make visual aids, such as poster board and markers
- ○◇ science notebook

Safety Note Please review and follow the safety guidelines at the beginning of this volume.

Procedure

1. Work with your partners to research the topic assigned by your teacher. Conduct your research on the Internet or in books on genetic engineering. Possible topics include the following:

gene cloning

gene therapy

genetically modified pork

genetically modified crops (such as corn, soybeans, and tomatoes)

genetically modified agrofuels

pharmaceuticals produced through recombinant DNA

transgenic fish for aquariums

transgenic fish for human consumption

prescreening embryos for diseases

human-animal hybrids

2. For the topic you are assigned, answer the following questions in detail:

   a. What is it? Introduce the topic with a paragraph.

   b. How is it done? Explain the procedure or process in detail, using diagrams or flow charts to clarify difficult points.

   c. What are the pros and cons? Discuss the social and ethical issues associated with this topic. Explain why some people are for it while others are opposed to it.

   d. What is the current status? What is being done today? Give some specific examples.

   e. What is planned for the future? What kind of work might we expect in the future?

3. Design a poster to reflect the answers to these questions. On the poster, include at least three drawings or pictures that help explain the topic. If needed, supplement your poster with charts, graphs, tables, or models.

4. Present you topic to the class. Your presentation should be creative and interesting and should last 5 to 10 minutes. Everyone in the group should have a role in the presentation.

5. Answer questions from the audience.

6. Write a one-page personal position paper on the topic that you presented. In the paper, explain your views on the topic and discuss how you arrived at those views.

7. When other groups present their topics, listen, take notes, and ask questions to help clarify your understanding.

Analysis

1. In your own words, define a gene.
2. How could genetic engineering help save human lives?
3. Based on what you learned in this lesson, how has genetic engineering changed agriculture?
4. Would you be for or against the development of a genetically engineered drought-resistant wheat plant? Explain your reasoning.

What's Going On?

Through genetic engineering, scientists have been successfully producing medications for more than 20 years. In 1982, scientists isolated the human insulin gene and inserted it into the DNA of *E. coli*, a common bacterium (see Figure 2). When the *E. coli* divided to form two cells, each new cell received a copy of the human insulin gene. After thousands of cell divisions, vats full of *E. coli* cells were producing large quantities of the protein insulin that was purified and sold to diabetics worldwide. Since that time, scientists have expanded their work to yield dozens of other pharmaceuticals. Genetically engineered human growth hormone is used to treat dwarfism in children. Epidermal growth factor speeds wound healing, interferon treats genital warts and some types of cancer, lung surfactant proteins help newborns with respiratory problems, and rennin inhibitor lowers blood pressure.

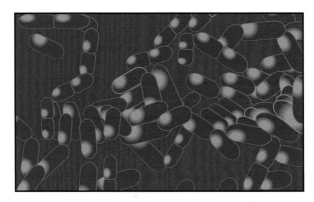

Figure 2

***E. coli* are rod-shaped bacteria found in the digestive systems of humans and other organisms.**

Connections

The DNA within your cells uses the same code as the DNA in cells of bacteria, oak trees, worms, and giraffes. All DNA is made up of two strands of nucleotides that are twisted into a double helix. Each nucleotide is made up of a phosphate group, the sugar deoxyribose, and one of four nitrogenous bases, adenine, guanine, cytosine, or thymine. The only difference in the DNA of different organisms is the order in which the bases are arranged. Whether in a person or a bacterium, there are three bases on a strand of DNA code for a particular protein. For example, the sequence of bases adenine-cytosine-uracil codes for the amino acid threonine. Proteins are made from long chains made up of hundred of amino acids. It is because of this universality of DNA's makeup that genetic engineering can be carried out.

Want to Know More?

See appendix for Our Findings.

Further Reading

American Society of Gene and Cell Therapy, 2009. Available online. URL: http://www.asgt.org/. Accessed January 23, 2010. Links on this Web site provide information on gene therapy.

GeneWatch UK. Available online. URL: http://www.genewatch.org/ index-396405. Accessed January 23, 2010. GeneWatch is concerned about the development of genetic technology and acts as a watchdog group to monitor the use and safety of gene technologies. Through this extensive Web site, students can gather information about a variety of products that result from genetic engineering.

Highfield, Roger. "Human-Pig Hybrid Embryos Given Go Ahead," *Telegraph*. January 7, 2008. Available online. URL: http://www.telegraph.co.uk/ earth/main.jhtml?view=DETAILS&grid=&xml=/earth/2008/07/01/ sciembryo101.xml. Accessed July 8, 2008. In this article, Highfield explains the reasons behind developing human-animal hybrids.

Maugh, Thomas H., II. "Gene Therapy Makes Major Stride in 'Lorenzo's Oil' Disease," *Los Angeles Times*, November 5, 2009. Available online. URL: http://www.latimes.com/features/health/la-sci-gene-therapy6-2009nov06,0,1848965.story. Accessed January 23, 2010. This article reports on the use of a deactivated HIV carrier, to successfully implant a normal gene into boys with adrenoleukodystrophy.

Rosenthal, Elisabeth. "A Genetically Modified Potato, Not for Eating, Is Stirring Some Opposition in Europe," *New York Times*, July 24, 2007. Available online. URL: http://www.nytimes.com/2007/07/24/business/worldbusiness/24spuds.html. Accessed January 23, 2010. In this article, Rosenthal discusses the problems encountered by growers of genetically modified food.

Sullivan, Dennis M. "Reproductive Technologies 101," Bioethics.com, February 14, 2007. Available online. URL: http://bioethics.com/?page_id=1733. Accessed July 8, 2008. Techniques behind embryo implantation are explained on this Web site.

Scope and Sequence Chart

This chart aligns the experiments in this book with some of the National Science Content Standards. (These experiments do not address every national science standard.) Please refer to your local and state content standards for additional information. As always, adult supervision is recommended and discretion should be used in selecting experiments appropriate to each age group or to individual students.

Standard	Grades 5–8	Grades 9–12
Physical Science		
Properties and changes of properties in matter		
Chemical reactions		
Motions and forces		
Transfer of energy and interactions of energy and matter		
Conservation of energy and increase in disorder		
Life Science		
Cells and structure and function in living systems	1, 2	1, 2
Reproduction and heredity	all	all
Regulation and behavior		

Standard	Grades 5–8	Grades 9–12
Populations and ecosystems		
Diversity and adaptations of organisms	4	4
Interdependence of organisms		
Matter, energy, and organization in living systems		
Biological evolution	2, 7, 11	2, 7, 11
Earth Science		
Structure and energy in the Earth system		
Geochemical cycles		
Origin and evolution of the Earth system		
Origin and evolution of the universe		
Earth in the solar system		
Nature of Science		
Science in history		
Science as an endeavor	all	all

Grade Level

Setting

The experiments are classified by materials and equipment use as follows:

- Those under SCHOOL LABORATORY involve materials and equipment found only in science laboratories. Those under SCHOOL LABORATORY must be carried out there under the supervision of the teacher or another adult.

- Those under HOME involve household or everyday materials. Some of these can be done at home, but call for supervision.

SCHOOL LABORATORY

7. Inheritance of Taste

9. Extracting DNA From Cheek Cells

12. The Traits of Parents and Offspring Are Not Identical

13. Transmission of Sex-linked Mutations

16. Introduction to Gel Electrophoresis

17. DNA Gel Electrophoresis

HOME

1. Cells in Mitosis

2. Amino Acids in Sickle Cell Anemia

3. Genetic Engineering With Plasmids

4. Meiosis

5. Inheritance of Traits

6. Predicted and Actual Results of Genetic Crosses

8. Using Karyotypes to Diagnose Conditions

10. Design an Organism's Traits

11. Chromosomal Mutations

Our Findings

1. CELLS IN MITOSIS

Idea for class discussion: Ask students to guess how many cells make up their bodies. The answer is "trillions!" Ask them where all of these cells come from.

Analysis

1. In an interphase cell, the nuclear membrane is present, chromatin is thin, and the nucleolus is visible.

2. Answers will vary. In prophase, the chromosomes have thickened and are visible and the nuclear membrane has disappeared.

3. In metaphase, chromosomes are lined up on the equator. In anaphase, chromosomes are no longer on the equator, but have moved toward the cell's poles. In telophase, the chromosomes are at the poles.

4. about 96 percent

5. interphase

6. Root cells are rapidly growing.

7. Answers will vary, but could include any rapidly growing tissue such as a dividing embryo or epidermal tissue.

2. AMINO ACIDS IN SICKLE CELL ANEMIA

Idea for class discussion: Review the basic steps of protein synthesis with the class, discussing DNA triplets, mRNA codons, nucleotides, and amino acid chains.

Analysis

1. The eleventh nucleotides are different; adenine is found in normal hemoglobin and thymine in sickle cell hemoglobin.

2. Normal hemoglobin produces a mRNA strand containing uracil at the eleventh position. Sickle cell hemoglobin will have adenine at the same position.

3. The fourth triplet on DNA of normal hemoglobin will produce valine; the same position on sickle cell hemoglobin will produce glutamic acid.

4. Glutamic acid changes the shape of the chain.

5. Glutamic acid is polar and has a charge.

6. Answers will vary. The oppositely charged amino acids would be attracted to each other.

7. Polar amino acids can attract or repel each other and cause the protein to bend.

3. GENETIC ENGINEERING WITH PLASMIDS

Idea for class discussion: Ask students to identify the source of insulin that diabetics buy from the pharmacy. If necessary discuss the fact that the pancreas makes insulin, a hormone that makes it possible for cells to take up glucose.

Notes to the teacher: The plasmid DNA should be cut at the following point:

A T A T C A   A G C T T C C C G A G A C T T A C C C C A G A <u>G A C A C G</u> A A A

The human DNA should be cut at the following points. The insulin DNA is highlighted.

A   A G C T T A A A A T A G C A T C C C T A G A A C A A C C C A   A G C T T

Analysis

1. Scissors represent a restriction enzyme.

2. Tape represents ligase.

3. no

4. The gene for antibiotic resistance is needed to separate bacterial cells that contain the plasmids from cells that do not.

5. c. The strip of white paper taped into the colored paper, these two pieces of paper represent the plasmid and the gene of interest.

6. Answers will vary. Bacteria and humans have the same genetic code.

7. Answers will vary. Several proteins are produced by recombinant DNA. In addition, genes can be transferred from one organism to another.

4. MEIOSIS

Idea for class discussion: Point out that human cells that undergo mitosis have 46 chromosomes. Ask students why fertilized eggs, which are made from the combination of two cells, do not have 92 chromosomes.

Analysis

1. 1
2. 2
3. 1
4. No. The chromosomes had experienced synapsis followed by sorting into gametes.
5. 4
6. 2
7. 1
8. No. The chromosomes had experienced synapsis followed by sorting into gametes.
9. Crossing over (synapsis) produces variation in offspring.

5. INHERITANCE OF TRAITS

Idea for class discussion: Have a few students describe some traits that are common in their families. For example, one family may have thin lips or a wide nose. Ask why everyone in the family does not display these common traits.

Analysis

1. 50 percent; 50 percent
2. 50 percent
3. 2
4. Answers will vary. The second offspring would have a different combination of traits because the results of coin flipping would have been different.
5. Wavy is an intermediate form between curly and straight and does not show the usual dominant or recessive mode of inheritance.

6. Answers will vary. Although two brothers have the same parents they are made from gametes that contain different combinations of traits.

7. Yes. Blue eyes are recessive, so both brown-eyed parents could carry the allele for blue eyes.

6. PREDICTED AND ACTUAL RESULTS OF GENETIC CROSSES

Idea for class discussion: Ask students why a dog breeder might want to be able to predict the offspring of a cross between two award-winning dogs.

Analysis

1. A Punnett square can be used to predict the chance that an offspring will show a particular combination of genes.

2. (a) BB: 25 percent; (b) Bb: 50 percent; (c) bb: 25 percent

3. (a) BB: 2.5; (b) Bb: 5; (c) bb: 2.5

4. Answers will vary. The actual and predicted numbers may not be very close because of the small sample size.

5. Answers will vary. Because of the larger sample size, the actual and predicted values may have been close.

7. INHERITANCE OF TASTE

Idea for class discussion: Discuss the evolutionary benefits of taste, including the ability to detect potential food items that might be poisonous. Point out that many plant toxins have a bitter taste.

Analysis

1. PTC paper is paper that contains the chemical phenylthiocarbamide.

2. Not everyone has the gene that enables them to taste PTC paper.

3. The control strip acts as a comparison to the PTC paper.

4. Answers will vary.

5. Answers will vary.

6. Answers will vary.

8. USING KARYOTYPES TO DIAGNOSE CONDITIONS

Idea for class discussion: Ask students to suggest some reasons why an individual might want to have his or her chromosomes examined.

Analysis

1. A couple might be concerned about the inheritance of a genetic disease.

2. Male karyotypes include XY and female karyotypes XX as chromosome pair 23.

3. 46; 23; 23

4. 46

5. 23

6. 44

7. Female; the individual has two X chromosomes.

8. There are three chromosome 21s in Figure 2; Figure 1 shows only two.

9. Down syndrome or trisomy 21

10. Figure 3 shows an individual with two Xs and one Y; Figure 1 is a normal female with two Xs.

9. EXTRACTING DNA FROM CHEEK CELLS

Idea for class discussion: Ask students to imagine that they are detectives. How might they collect DNA samples from suspects?

Analysis

1. DNA, or deoxyribonucleic acid, is the molecule that carries genetic information.

2. Individuals inherit DNA from their parents.

3. A nucleotide has three parts: a nitrogen base, a phosphate group, and a sugar.

4. Answers will vary. The DNA is a white, gelatinous mass.

5. The DNA in this experiment came from cheek cells.

6. Answers will vary but could include skin cells, the root of hair, bone cells, and white blood cells.

10. DESIGN AN ORGANISM'S TRAITS

Idea for class discussion: Have students suggest some definitions for *dominant trait, recessive trait,* and *codominant trait*.

Analysis

1. simple dominance

2. Codominant traits are both expressed; incompletely dominant traits blend.

3. Males have only one X chromosome, so if they have a recessive trait it will be expressed. Females have two X chromosomes, and they often have a dominant trait on one that masks the presence of a recessive trait.

4. Index cards represented chromosomes.

5. Letters written on both sides of the index cards represented genes.

6. Answers will vary. The types of inheritance studied in this lab are found in humans and many other organisms.

11. CHROMOSOMAL MUTATIONS

Idea for class discussion: Discuss with students the potential for genetic damage in an individual who has the wrong number of chromosomes or chromosomes that have been changed.

Analysis

1. deletions and translocations

2. Without its adjacent promoter, a gene might not be able to function.

3. Chromosomal mutations cause more damage to the organism than point mutations because they involve many genes.

4. Answers will vary. A deletion causes more severe changes than a translocation because genetic material is lost.

12. THE TRAITS OF PARENTS AND OFFSPRING ARE NOT IDENTICAL

Idea for class discussion: Ask students why they do not look exactly like their parents. Elicit the idea that the genes of offspring are a combination of the genes of their parents.

Analysis

1. Letters used may vary. First cross between parent generations is shown in Figure 1a below; Second cross of F1 generation flies is shown in Figure 1b:

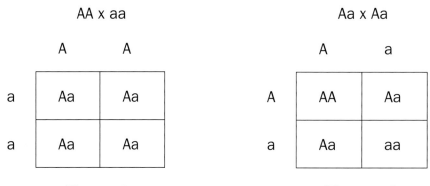

AA x aa   Aa x Aa

	A	A
a	Aa	Aa
a	Aa	Aa

	A	a
A	AA	Aa
a	Aa	aa

Figure 1a   **Figure 1b**

2. Student answers will vary based on laboratory data.

3. Student answers will vary based on their results. Answers should include an explanation of why their data agreed with the expected results or why it did not.

4. Answers will vary based on class data. Generally the percentages will be closer to 75 percent wild type and 25 percent mutant than the individual results were.

5. Answers will vary based on results. Usually the results are closer to the expected values with a larger sample size.

6. The difference between the results in a small sample size and the expected results should be greater. Error is higher in small sample sizes.

7. In a larger population, there is less deviation from the expected values because there are more organisms to calculate into the average. Therefore, the results are closer to the normal value since any of the organisms that did not behave as expected will be "canceled out" by the large number of other individuals.

13. TRANSMISSION OF SEX-LINKED MUTATIONS

Idea for class discussion: Point out that red-green color blindness is more common in males than females. Ask students to offer some explanations for this fact.

Analysis

1. First cross is shown in Figure 2a below; Second cross is shown in Figure 2b.

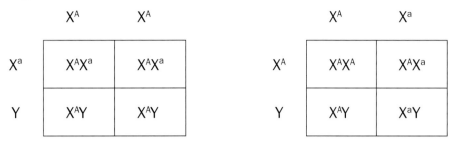

	X^A	X^A
X^a	X^AX^a	X^AX^a
Y	X^AY	X^AY

	X^A	X^a
X^A	X^AX^A	X^AX^a
Y	X^AY	X^aY

Figure 2a   **Figure 2b**

2. All of the flies have the wild-type phenotype. It is impossible to tell which individuals are carriers of the trait, because all of them appear to be wild type. However, in this F1 generation, all of the females are carriers of the trait.

3. Answers will vary based on laboratory results. Students should provide an explanation of why their data agreed with the predictions or why it did not.

4. Sex-linked traits are found more often in the male offspring than in females. Autosomal traits appear equally in both males and females.

5. Females can express sex-linked traits, but they are much more common in males. No females should have been found to have the trait in this experiment. In order for a female to have the trait, a mutant male must be crossed with a heterozygous female carrier. When this cross is performed, it is expected that 50 percent of the females and 50 percent of the males will express the trait.

6. The Punnett square is shown in Figure 3 below. Although the parent phenotypes are the same as the first cross in this laboratory, the genotypes are different. Therefore, half of the males and half of the females are expected to express the recessive sex-linked trait in this case.

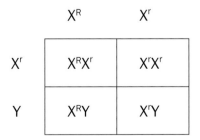

	X^R	X^r
X^r	X^RX^r	X^rX^r
Y	X^RY	X^rY

Figure 3

14. PEDIGREES SHOW TRAITS WITHIN FAMILIES

Idea for class discussion: Show students a simple pedigree and ask them what it tells them.

Analysis

1. Pedigree is shown in Figure 4 below. (Student answers could be different.)

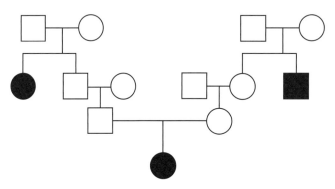

Figure 4

2. Pedigree is shown in Figure 5 below.

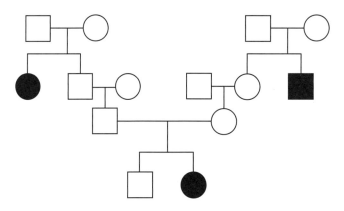

Figure 5

3. The Punnett square is shown in Figure 6 below. S represents the normal genotype and s is the recessive gene for sickle cell anemia. Shawn is not ss because he does not have the gene. Therefore, there is a 2:1 probability that he is a carrier and has the genotype Ss.

	S	s
S	SS	Ss
s	Ss	ss

Figure 6

4. There is 0 percent chance. Since Erin is not a carrier, none of Shawn and Erin's children will have sickle cell anemia. (In the Punnett square [Figure 7 below], Erin's genes are on the top and Shawn's on the side.)

	S	S
S	SS	SS
s	Ss	Ss

Figure 7

5. (a) autosomal dominant. The trait shows up in every generation; (b) granddaughter; (c) Individual 1 is heterozygous for the trait.

15. MODEL OF A DNA MOLECULE

Idea for class discussion: Review the components of a nucleotide and the fact that DNA is a double chain of nucleotides.

Analysis

1. DNA is the nucleic acid that carries an individual's genetic information.

2. DNA is located in the nuclei of cells.

3. deoxyribose, a phosphate group, and a nitrogenous base

4. Adenine and guanine are large bases; when paired, they do not fit in a DNA molecule.

5. The sequence of bases in DNA is slightly different in individuals.

16. INTRODUCTION TO GEL ELECTROPHORESIS

Idea for class discussion: Ask students to suggest some ways to separate different molecules in a mixture.

Notes to the teacher: Prepare an unknown dye by mixing two or more of the known dyes. To prepare 0.8 percent agarose gel for electrophoresis, in 250 milliliter (ml) Pyrex™ bottle combine: 125 ml 1X TBE and 1 gram (g) agarose. Microwave uncovered to melt agarose. Be careful not to boil over. Cover loosely and store at room temperature. Remelt when needed. Gels can be made a day or two before the experiment and stored in the refrigerator. The voltage will vary depending on the size of the chamber. The general rule is a maximum of 5 volts (V) per centimeter of distance between the two electrodes. For example, if the distance between electrodes is 10 centimeters (cm), the electrophoresis chamber should be run at 50 V. If the gel is run at a higher voltage, it may melt the agarose. If necessary, gels can be run for much longer (even overnight) on low voltage with good results.

Analysis

1. The buffer conducts the electric current through the gel.

2. Orange G, xylene cyanol, and bromthymol blue move toward the positive pole. Safranin O and Janus green move toward the negative pole.

3. Bromthymol blue has a negative charge. Janus green has a positive charge.

4. Orange G; It migrated about 30 millimeters (mm).

5. Answers will vary based on the teacher's preparation of the unknown dye.

17. DNA GEL ELECTROPHORESIS

Idea for class discussion: Ask students to discuss what they know about making a DNA fingerprint.

Notes to the teacher. Prepare five microtubes per lab group, adding restrictive enzymes as shown below. Label the tubes 1 through 4 and X. Keep the restriction enzymes cold until used.

Microtube	Material in microtubes
1	Add nothing to this microtube.
2	1 µL of *Hind*III
3	1 µL of *Bam*HI
4	1 µL of *Eco*RI
X	1 µL of *Bam*HI

To prepare 0.8 percent agarose gel for electrophoresis, in 250 ml Pyrex™ bottle, combine: 125 ml 1X TBE and 1 g agarose. Microwave uncovered to melt agarose. Be careful not to boil over. Cover loosely and store at room temperature. Remelt when needed. The voltage will vary depending on the size of the electrophoresis chamber. The general rule is a maximum of 5 V per centimeter of distance between the two electrodes. For example, if the distance between electrodes is 10 cm, the electrophoresis chamber should be run at 50 V. If the gel is run at a higher voltage, it may melt the agarose. If necessary, gels can be run for much longer (even overnight) on low voltage with good results. After the power is turned off, the gel can stay in the chamber for several hours before staining.

Analysis

1. The DNA in microtubes 2 and 3 was cut with different restriction enzymes.

2. Microtube 3 and microtube X have the same banding pattern.

3. *Bam*III was used in microtube X; it has the same pattern as microtube 3, which is known to contain *Bam*III.

4. The R_f indicates the relative size of the fragment and can be used to calculate the number of base pairs.

18. CONTROL OF GENE EXPRESSION

Idea for class discussion: Every cell contains the same DNA. Genes on an individual's DNA code for the production of thousands of different proteins. However, every cell in the body does not produce every protein. For example, skin does not produce hemoglobin and brain cells do not make insulin. Ask students to offer some explanations for this.

Analysis

1. Transcription is the process in which the DNA code is copied to make a strand of mRNA.

2. No. The repressor is in the way.

3. No. The inducer physically prevents the repressor from binding.

4. No.

5. transcription

6. Answers will vary. When lactose it present, it binds to the repressor and prevents it from interfering with RNA polymerase.

19. GENETICS LEARNING CENTERS

Idea for class discussion: Discuss the concept of mode of inheritance; find out what students already understand on the topic.

Analysis

1. (a) X-linked dominant; (b) autosomal dominant; (c) autosomal recessive; (d) X-linked dominant; (e) mitochondrial; (f) X-linked recessive; (g) autosomal dominant

2. (a) X-linked dominant; (b) codominant; (c) autosomal recessive; (d) autosomal dominant

3. (a) autosomal recessive; (b) mitochondrial; (c) autosomal dominant

20. GENETIC ENGINEERING PRESENTATION

Idea for class discussion: If possible, show students a genetically engineered fruit or vegetable or a picture of a genetically engineered fruit or vegetable. (Genetically engineered produce is marked with special stickers.) Without telling students why, ask them if there is anything unusual about the way the food looks. Point out that the food may be very similar in appearance to products that are not genetically engineered, but it may carry a gene that prevents frost damage, introduces insect resistance, or creates some other desirable trait.

Analysis

1. Answers will vary. A gene is a section of DNA that codes for a particular protein.

2. Answers will vary. Genetic engineering produces life-saving medications as well as a few animal organs (such as heart valves) that can be used by humans.

3. Answers will vary. Genetic engineering has produced plants that are resistant to insects, herbicides, drought, and frost.

4. Answers will vary based on students' opinions of the pros and cons of genetic engineering.

Glossary

agarose gel semisolid material used to separate molecules in gel electrophoresis

allele one of the forms or versions of a gene found at a particular point on a chromosome

amniocentesis medical procedure during which a small sample of amniotic fluid is removed from a pregnant woman so that the fetus's chromosomes can be examined for genetic disease

anemia condition in which the blood cannot transport the normal amount of oxygen either due to lack of red blood cells or lack of hemoglobin

antibody protein in the body that is produced in response to a particular antigen

antigen substance such as a bacterium, virus, or pollen that stimulates an immune response and leads to the production of antibodies

autosome any chromosome that is not involved in determining an individual's sex

benign not invading other tissue in the body; not dangerous

buccal cells cells on the inside of the cheek

cancer an abnormal growth caused by uncontrolled cell division

cellular respiration aerobic process in which glucose is changed to a usable form of energy called ATP

centrioles pair of barrel-shaped organelles found in animal and fungal cells that play a role in cell division

centromere region of a chromosome that appears during cell division where sister chromatids are held together

chemotherapy treatment of cancer and other diseases using chemicals that kill cells

chorionic villus sampling prenatal test in which part of the placenta is removed so that the fetus's chromosomes can be examined for genetic disease

chromatin protein and DNA within a cell's nucleus from which chromosomes condense during cell division

chromosome strand of DNA that has coiled and condensed in preparation of cell division

cleavage the repeated cell divisions of a fertilized egg

codominance condition in which both genes in an allelic pairs are expressed with neither being dominant

codon set of three nucleotides on messenger RNA that codes for a particular amino acid

covalent bond type of bond between atoms in which electrons are shared

cri du chat syndrome genetic disorder caused by the loss of a portion of chromosome 5 that causes mental retardation, small head size, loss of muscle tone, and a catlike cry

cytokinesis division of a cell following replication and division of its chromosomes

deletion mutation in which all or part of a chromosome is missing

de novo   of a change in a gene that is present for the first time

deoxyribonucleic acid (DNA)   genetic material found within a cell

diploid   of a cell containing a complete set of chromosomes, such as a body cell

dominant trait   genetic trait that hides the expression of a recessive trait

duplication   mutation in which part or all of a chromosome is duplicated

enzyme   chemical within living things that speeds up or slows down reactions

epithelial cells   closely packed cells that cover surfaces and line cavities of the body

erythrocyte   red blood cell; hemoglobin-containing cell in the blood that transports oxygen

F1 generation   offspring of a cross between two individuals of the parental generation

F2 generation   offspring of a cross between two individuals of the F1 generation

fertilization   fusion of egg and sperm

gamete   sex cell, either egg or sperm

gel electrophoresis   procedure in which molecules such as protein or DNA are separated by the rate at which they pass through a gel

gene   section of DNA that codes for a particular trait

gene cloning   process of isolating a particular gene of interest and making copies of it

genetic engineering   set of techniques used to manipulate the DNA of organisms

geneticist   scientist who studies inheritance, the way traits are passed from one generation to the next

genotype   the genes of an organism

haploid   of a cell containing half a set of chromosomes, such as a sperm or an egg

herbicide   chemical used to kill unwanted plants

hermaphrodite   individual that possess both male and female sex organs

heterozygote (hybrid)   an organism that has different alleles of a gene

homologous chromosomes (homologues)   chromosomes of similar shape and size that pair during meiosis

homozygote   an organism that has the same alleles of a gene on both chromosomes

hydrogen bond   weak bond between a slightly positively charged hydrogen atom of one molecule and a slightly negatively charged atom in another molecule

incomplete dominance   type of inheritance in which alleles interact to produce an intermediate phenotype

insulin   protein produced by cells in the pancreas that regulates the uptake of glucose by cells

interphase   part of the cell cycle during which cells grow

inversion   type of mutation in which part of a chromosome detaches, then reattaches in an upside position

karyotype   photograph of an individual's chromosomes showing their size and shape

lac operon   operon in *E. coli* that controls the breakdown of lactose

lactase   enzyme that breaks down lactose into simpler sugars

law of segregation   Mandel's law stating that pairs of alleles separate randomly when gametes are formed

ligase   type of enzyme that causes the binding of molecules

ligation the process of binding molecules

malignant invasive or able to spread throughout the body; dangerous

meiosis type of cell division in which gametes are produced

menopause the time when a woman's reproductive cycle ends

microcephaly condition in which an individual has a small head due to lack of development of the brain

midpiece section of a sperm cell located between the head and tail that contains mitochondria

mitochondrial DNA small ring of DNA found within mitochondria

mitosis type of cell division responsible for growth and repairs in which diploid cells are produced

mitotic spindle system of microtubules in eukaryotic cells that separates chromosomes during cell division

motile able to move

mutation any change in the DNA of an organism

nucleic acid macromolecule made up of chains of nucleotides, including RNA and DNA

nucleotide monomer of a nucleic acid made up of a nitrogenous base, sugar, and phosphate group

oogenesis the process of gamete production in a female

oogonium an immature egg cell, present in the ovary

operator gene that controls the expression of other genes

organelle structure within a cell that has a specialized function

oviduct tube that carries a newly released egg cell from the ovary to the uterus

ovipositor tube-shaped abdominal organ in some female insects that is used to lay eggs

parthenogenesis process in which an unfertilized egg divides and undergoes development

pedigree chart that shows the inheritance of a trait within a family

phenotype the way an organism looks based on its genotype

placenta organ that connects a developing fetus to the mother's uterus

plasmid small, circular piece of DNA found in prokaryotic cells

point mutation type of mutation that causes a change in a single base on a strand of DNA

polypeptide short string of amino acids that are held together by peptide bonds

polyploidy condition of having more than the diploid number of chromosomes

probability the likelihood that an event will occur

prokaryote one-celled organism that lacks a nucleus and membrane-bound organelles

promoter region of DNA that aids in the transcription of a gene

puberty time of life in which the reproductive glands become active

Punnett square diagram used to predict the possible offspring of a genetic cross

purine nitrogenous base that has a double-ring structure such as adenine and guanine

pyrimidine   nitrogenous base that has a single-ring structure such as thymine and adenine

radiation therapy   treatment of disease using high-energy radiation to kill invasive cells

recessive trait   trait that is not expressed if a dominant trait is present

reciprocal translocation   type of mutation in which a section of DNA is swapped between nonhomologous chromosomes

recombinant DNA   genetically engineered DNA formed by combining DNA from two different organisms

restriction enzyme   protein that recognizes a short sequence of DNA and cuts the strand at that location to yield restriction fragments

restriction fragment length polymorphism (RFLP)   variations in individuals of DNA fragments cut with restriction enzymes

ribonucleic acid (RNA)   single-stranded form of nucleic acid found primarily in the cytoplasm that plays a role in protein synthesis

ribosome   organelle found in all types of cells that facilitates the translation of messenger RNA into protein

RNA polymerase   enzyme that speeds up the production of a strand of RNA from DNA

roan   coat color found in horses and cattle that is a mixture of white and brown hairs

sex combs   bristles on the front legs of male fruit flies used to grip females during mating

sex-linked   related to genes that are carried on the sex chromosomes

sister chromatids   identical copies of chromosomes that are bound by a centromere

spermatogenesis   process of sperm production in the testes

synapsis   process of pairing of two homologous chromosomes during meiosis

test cross   cross between an organism of unknown genotype for a particular trait and an organism that is homozygous recessive for that trait

tetrad   group of four chromatids formed when two replicated homologous chromosomes pair in meiosis

transcription   process in which the DNA genetic code is used to make a strand of messenger RNA

transcription factors   proteins that catalyze the production of RNA in eukaryotic cells

translation   process in which a strand of messenger RNA attaches to a ribosome and creates a protein

translocation   type of mutation caused by the rearrangement of parts of nonhomologous chromosomes

trisomy   chromosomal abnormality in which there is an extra chromosome

ultrasound   high-frequency sound wave that can be reflected from tissue and used to generate a picture

X-ray   high-energy electromagnetic radiation used in medical imaging

Internet Resources

The World Wide Web is an invaluable source of information for students, teachers, and parents. The following list is intended to help you get started exploring educational sites that relate to the book. It is just a sample of the Web material that is available to you. All of these sites were accessible as of June 2010.

Educational Resources

Blumberg, Robert B. MendelWeb. Available online. URL: http://www.mendelweb.org/MWtoc.html. Accessed February 6, 2010. This Web site provides links to dozens of pages related to Gregor Mendel and his work in genetics.

"Cytogenetics and Chromosomal Disorders," December 8, 1996. Available online. URL: http://arbl.cvmbs.colostate.edu/hbooks/genetics/medgen/chromo/index.html. Accessed February 6, 2010. An excellent explanation of abnormal chromosome numbers is presented on this Web site.

DNA From the Beginning, 2002. Available online. URL: http://www.dnaftb.org/dnaftb/. Accessed January 20, 2010. This primer on basic DNA, genetics, and heredity, provided by Cold Springs Harbor laboratory, includes a discussion of gene control.

Dolan DNA Learning Center. Available online. URL: http://www.dnalc.org/resources/animations/gelelectrophoresis.html. Accessed February 6, 2010. Provided by the Cold Springs Harbor Laboratory, this Web site provides animations on gel electrophoresis and other topics related to DNA structure.

Genetics Home Reference, January 31, 2010. Available online. URL: http://ghr.nlm.nih.gov/handbook. Accessed February 6, 2010. This Web site provides information on cells, DNA, and genetic conditions.

Human Genome Project Information. "How Many Genes are in the Human Genome?" September 19, 2008. U.S. Department of Energy Office of Science. Available online. URL: http://www.ornl.gov/sci/techresources/Human_Genome/faq/genenumber.shtml. Accessed February 6, 2010. When the Human Genome Project finished analyzing human DNA in 2003, more than 24,000 protein-encoding genes had been found. However, ongoing research provides a continuous stream of new information, which is discussed on this Web site.

"Inside the Cell," 2005. National Institute of General Medical Sciences. Available online. URL: http://publications.nigms.nih.gov/insidethecell/. Accessed February 6, 2010. Functions of organelles, cell division, and aging are some of the topics discussed on this interesting Web site, which explains how cells work.

"Issues in Genomics," 2010. American Institute of Biological Sciences. Available online. URL: http://www.actionbioscience.org/genomic/index.html. Accessed February 6, 2010. This fantastic Web site provides links to articles on ethical issues related to genetics.

"The Lac Operon," July 9, 1998. BioTech Education. Available online. URL: http://biotech.icmb.utexas.edu/pages/science/lac_operon.html. Accessed February 6, 2010. This Web site explains how the regions of the lac operon play a role in controlling gene expression.

National Heart, Lung, and Blood Institute. "Sickle Cell Anemia." Available online. URL: http://www.nhlbi.nih.gov/health/dci/Diseases/Sca/SCA_SignsAndSymptoms.html. Accessed February 6, 2010. This Web site explains the symptoms and complications of sickle cell disease.

OMIM-Online Mendelian Inheritance in Man. National Center for Biotechnology Information. Available online. URL: http://www.ncbi.nlm.nih.gov/entrez/query.fcgi?db=OMIM. Accessed February 6, 2010. This Web site is an extensive database on genetic disorders.

"Sickle Cell Disease," 2009. Blood Diseases, University of Maryland. Available online. URL: http://www.umm.edu/blood/sickle.htm. Accessed November 15, 2009. This Web site discusses the causes and treatments of sickle cell disease.

Index

A

adenosine triphosphate (ATP) 7
agarose gel 100, 101, 103, 107, 109, 111
albinism 78
allele 28, 29, 31, 34, 35, 37, 41, 45, 58, 61, 64, 73, 91, 125
alpha1 antitrypsin deficiency 124
anemia 12
antibiotic resistance 15, 17-19
antibody 125
antigen 125

B

Bacillus thuringiensis 125
benign tumor 6
blood type 64
BRCA1 5
buccal swab 56

C

cancer 5, 6
cellular respiration 7
Chargaff, Erwin 98
chemotherapy 6
chorionic villus sampling 52
chromosome 1-3,
codominance 32, 58, 60-63, 120
Coffin-Lowry 124
covalent bond 19
Crick, Francis 98
cri du chat syndrome 71
CTNND2 71

cystic fibrosis 32, 78, 122, 124
cytokinesis 1, 21

D

deletion 67, 68, 71
deoxyribonucleic acid (DNA) 5, 7-9, 15-19, 21, 34, 44, 53, 55, 56, 66, 67, 71, 73, 78, 80, 93-97, 100, 104, 106-111, 113, 116, 119, 127, 120, 131
dominant 28-32, 34, 43, 58, 60-64, 73, 77, 78, 84, 87, 89, 90, 118-120, 122, 124, 125
Down syndrome 47, 51
Duchene muscular dystrophy 124
duplication 67, 68

E

erythrocyte 7
Escherichia coli 113

F

fertilization 26, 39, 124
Fox, Arthur 41
fragile X syndrome 122, 124
Franklin, Rosalind 98
fruit flies 73-75, 80, 81, 84

G

gamete 21
gel electrophoresis 100, 106
genetic engineering 18, 127, 130

genotype 11, 28, 29, 31, 34, 36-38, 58, 60-62, 73, 78
guinea pigs 35-38

H

hemoglobin 7-9, 12, 13
hemophilia 64, 124
herbicide 127
hermaphrodite 86
homologous chromosome (homolog) 21-23, 47
Huntington's disease 32, 122, 124
hydrogen bond 93

I

incomplete dominance 32, 45, 58, 60-64
insulin 15, 17-19, 113, 130
inversion 67, 70

K

karyotype 47, 48, 51
Klinefelter's syndrome 47, 51

L

lac operon 113, 114
lactose 113, 116
law of segregation 77
Leber hereditary optic neuropathy 125

M

malignant tumor 5
Marfan syndrome 32
meiosis 21, 22, 24, 25, 52, 78
Mendel, Gregor 28, 32, 34, 35, 39, 77